LEARN TO CROCH

MW01602527

LEARN TO CROCHET IN JUST ONE DAY AND CREATE QUICK AND EASY CROCHET PROJECTS

By Florence Schultz

TABLE OF CONTENTS

Crochet is an art form and an enjoyable and productive hobby. Crochet artists from around the world enjoy sharing and discovering new patterns. You can learn how to crochet in just one day and begin working easy and quick projects. In this book we will learn the basics of yarn and hooks, basic and a few intermediate crochet stitches, and the crochet techniques you need to learn to begin your lifelong journey with crochet.

There are several theories about the origin of crochet. Annie Potter, an American crochet expert wrote "The modern art of true crochet as we know it today was developed during the 16th century." She goes on to report crochet became known as 'crochet lace' in France and 'chain lace' in England. She also sites that in 1916 Walter Edmund Roth found examples of true crochet when he visited the Guiana Indians.

Lis Paludan of Denmark, who researched the origins of crochet in Europe, reported that the craft originated in Arabia and later spread along the trade routes to Tibet, Spain, and other Mediterranean countries. She also speculates crochet may have begun in a primitive tribe in South America, or may have begun in China.

Examples of crochet in Europe have been found as far back as the 1500's when it was known as 'nun's work' or 'nun's lace'. The crochet we know today was very popular in the 1800's in Europe. The beautiful and intricate art of Irish crochet saved many families from starvation during the potato famine in the mid-19th Century. No matter when or how crochet came into the world, today it is one of the most popular yarn arts and is gaining popularity with all age groups.

With this book you will join the ranks of crochet artists down through the centuries and learn a craft which gives you a chance to not only express your creativity, but create beautiful projects for yourself, friends, and family.

In this chapter we'll learn all about yarn and hooks. Choosing the correct yarn and hook for your project is essential, and in this chapter we'll learn just what you need to know to do this.

Yarn Fibers

Yarn is manufactured from three main types of fibers; animal, plant, and synthetic. Animal fibers include wool, alpaca, mohair, cashmere, and silk. Plant fibers include cotton, linen, hemp, bamboo, and soy. Synthetic yarn is produced from acrylic, polyesters, micro-fiber, and metallic threads. Each type of yarn offers benefits and a different type of stitch definition and drape.

Animal and plant yarns look best if they are blocked after you finish your project. Blocking stretches the yarn fibers and opens up the stitches. Wet the fabric and then roll it up in a large fluffy towel to remove most of the moisture. Do not ring the crocheted fabric or you will damage the stitches. Lay the fabric out on blocking pads or another large towel and pin the edges gently stretching the project into shape. Let it dry completely before you remove it.

You can also use a spray bottle for smaller projects. Pin the project out first and then lightly mist it and let dry.

Yarn Weights and Texture

Yarn comes in many different weights and textures. Yarn can range from very fine to very thick and bulky. Weights range from 0 to 7. Size 0 is the finest, while size 7 is the thickest.

A yarn's weight will affect the gauge of the stitches. Gauge refers to how many stitches in a row and how many rows it takes to make a four inch crochet swatch of fabric. It is important to check the gauge before you work a pattern. Use the recommended hook size and yarn weight and crochet up a small swatch of fabric.

Count the stitches across four inches and how many rows it takes to make four inches. This is the gauge. If your swatch is too large, go down a hook size. If your swatch is too small, go up a hook size.

You can substitute yarn in a pattern as long as it is the same weight and get the desired results.

Yarn Weight Chart			
Weight	Description	Recommended Hook	Stitches in 4"
0 Lace	Fingerling, Size 10 Crochet Thread	Steel 1.6-1.4mm/B-1	32-48
1 Superfine	Sock, Fingerling	2.25-3mm/B-1 to E-4	21-32
2 Fine	Sport, Baby	3.4-4.5mm/E-4 to 7	16-20
3 Light	DK, Light Worsted	4.5-5.5mm/7 to I/9	12-17
4 Medium	Worsted, Afghan, Aran	5.5-6.5mm/I-9 to K-10 ½	11-14
5 Bulky	Chunky, Craft, Rug	6.5-9mm/K-10 ½ to M-13	8-11
6 Super Bulky	Super Bulky, Roving	9-15mm/m-13 to Q	7-9
7 Jumbo	Jumbo, Roving	15mm and up	6 or less

In this table you can see a four-inch swatch of crocheted fabric done up with a medium weight yarn and a size I/9 hook will give you approximately 11 to 15 stiches across a four inches in a row. The same four inches with a fine yarn and a size E/4 hook gives you many more stitches; 16 to 20, so it is important to use the correct weight and hook size when working a pattern.

Understanding a Yarn Label

The yarn label contains important information you need to select the correct yarn for your next project. On the yarn label you will find the fiber content, color, weight, recommended hook size, gauge for that hook size, and laundry care symbols. I've included a list of laundry care symbols from the Lion Brand website for your reference in the back of this book.

In the following example we can see that this label is from a skein of Red Heart Super Save yarn in Cherry Red. It is acrylic yarn and had has a weight of 4. The recommended hook size is I/9 and this will give us an approximate gauge of 12 stitches and 15 rows in a four by four-inch swatch of crochet fabric. According to the laundry care symbols this yarn may be machine washed and dried, but not ironed. There is no dye lot, but if there were you would want to purchase enough of the same dye lot so the color is consistent in your project.

Crochet Hooks

Crochet hooks are pretty straightforward. You can find them with tapered or inline heads. Tapered heads are curved, while inline hooks have sharper edges. Both types of hooks produce the same exact stitches, so which one you use is a personal preference.

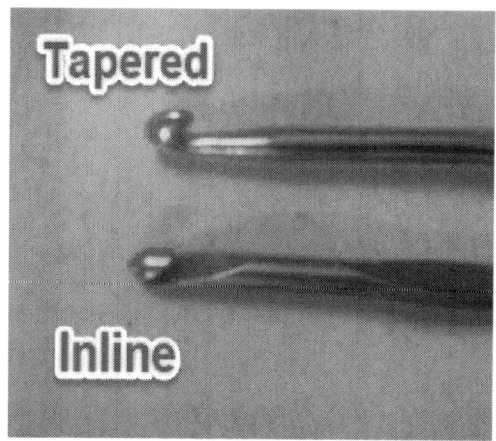

You can find crochet hooks made from aluminum, steel, bamboo, wood, plastic, and even antique bone hooks. Steel hooks are very fine hooks used with thread. Most jumbo hooks are made from plastic and are used for very large projects such as rugs. The majority of hooks sold in the US are made of aluminum or bamboo.

I recommend purchasing a good quality set of aluminum or bamboo hooks in sizes ranging from E to K. You can find these sets in most craft and big-box stores, or online.

Ergonomic hooks offer ease of use and comfort for those who have a hard time holding a regular hook. These types of hooks may have soft plastic or hard ceramic handles. You can also find ergonomic handles which fit onto your hooks which make them more comfortable and easy to use.

You will usually find hooks with a letter and number designation in the US. Hooks from the UK and other places may have millimeter or number designations.

US Hook Sizes			
US Size	Millimeter Size	US Size	Millimeter Size
B/1	2.25mm	J/10	6mm
C/2	2.75mm	K/10 ½	6.5mm
D/3	3.25mm	L/11	8mm
E/4	3.5mm	M-N/13	9mm

F/5	3.75mm	N-P/15	10mm
G/6	4mm	P/Q	15mm
7	4.5mm	Q	16mm
H/8	5mm	S	19mm
I/9	5.5mm		

Refer to the Reference Tables section in the back of the book for a complete list of crochet hook sizes.

Holding Your Hook

There are two main ways to hold a crochet hook: the pencil hold and the knife hold. Both create the same stitches so experiment with them to see which hold feels the most natural.

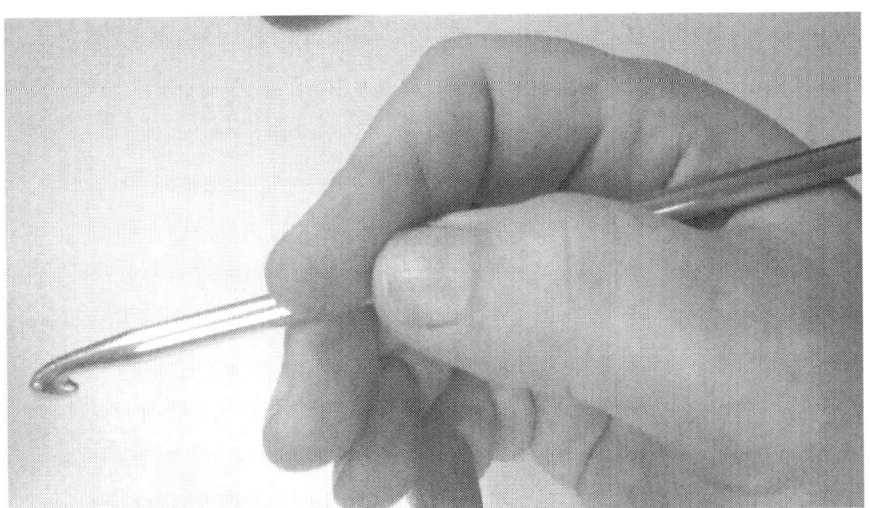

Pencil Hold

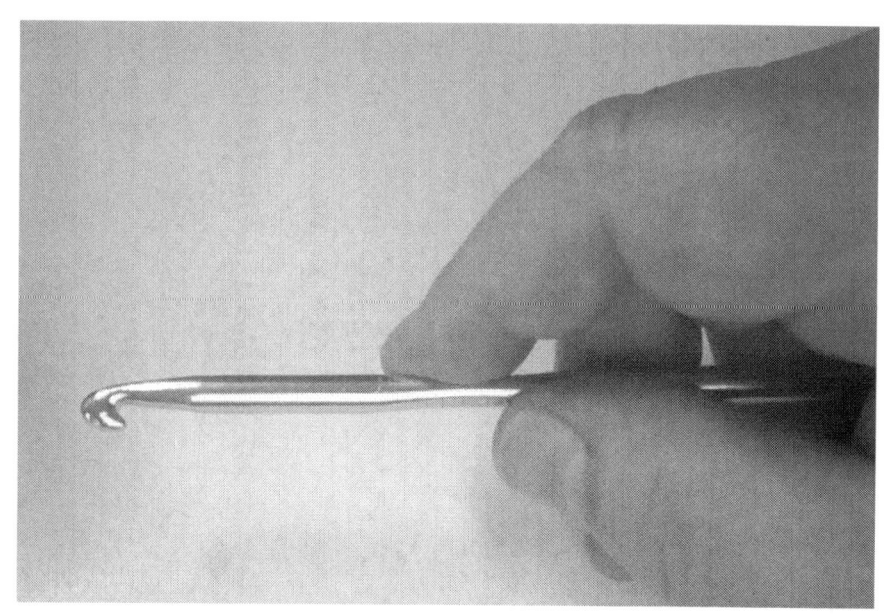

Knife Hold

In this chapter we will learn the basic crochet stitches you need to know to work patterns and create lovely crochet projects. These are stitches which are the basis for more complex stitches. Concentrate on getting used to handling the hook and yarn. Also concentrate on crocheting the stitches evenly. Tension is important in crochet so that your fabric is nice and even.

Count the stitches as you go. Crochet is based on stitch count, and yes, math. Don't worry it's not complicated math, but you need to be able to keep track of where you are in a pattern and be able to figure out pattern repeats and stitch counts. So, take your time and enjoy learning these stitches.

Chain Stitch

The first step is to create a slip knot and place it on your hook. Pull the yarn through the loop on the hook. This is the first chain stitch. Pull the yarn through the loop on the hook again, this is the second chain stitch. Practice chain stitches until they are all nice and even.

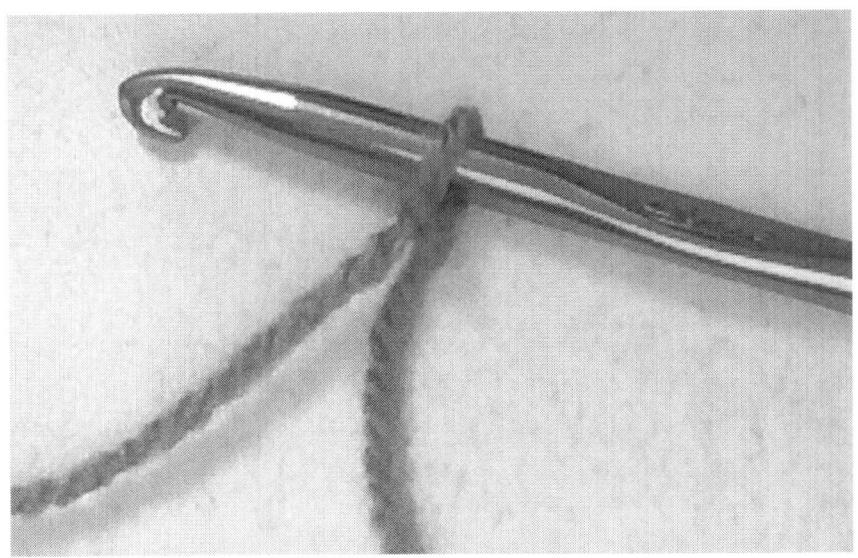

Slip Knot

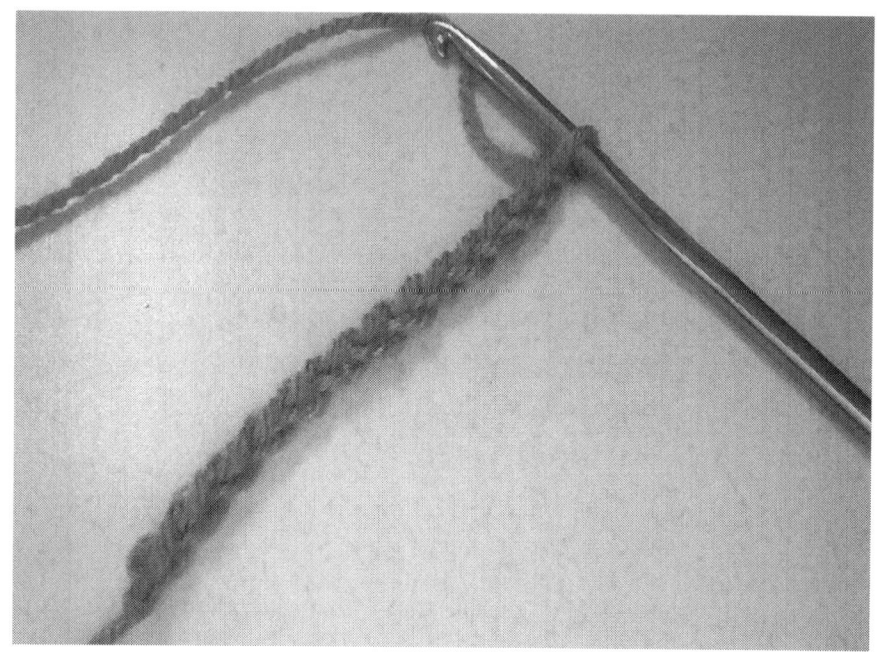

Completed Chain

Single Crochet

Single crochet stitches create a dense fabric. If you are beginning your first row with single crochet insert the hook into the second chain stitch from the hook. (The first chain counts as the first single crochet stitch.) Yarn over and pull the yarn through the chain stitch. Yarn over and pull through the two loops on the hook. This is a single crochet stitch. When you begin a new row with single crochet chain one. This counts as the first stitch. Insert the hook into the next stitch, yarn over and pull through, yarn over and pull through both loops on the hook.

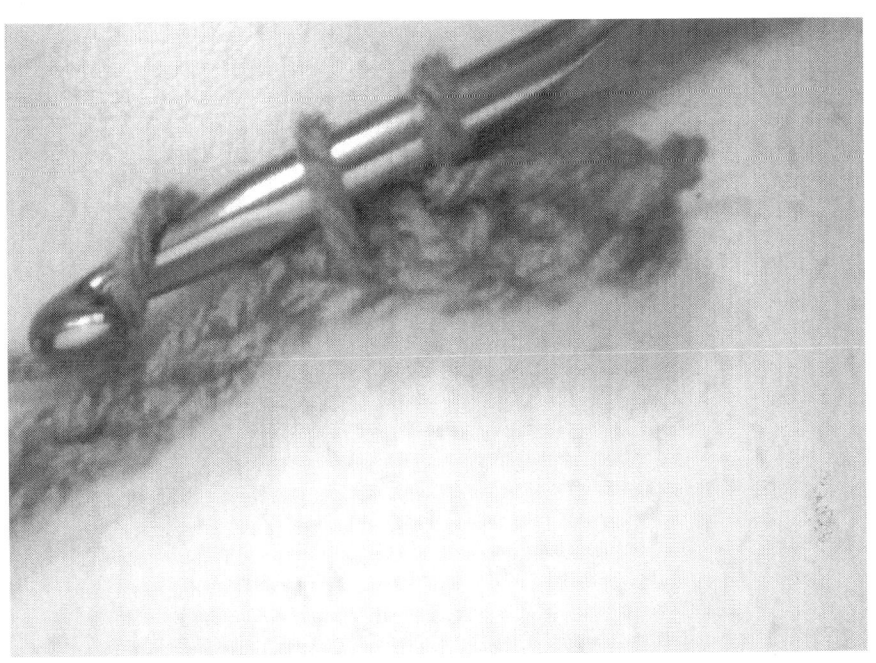

Insert the hook into the next stitch and yarn over

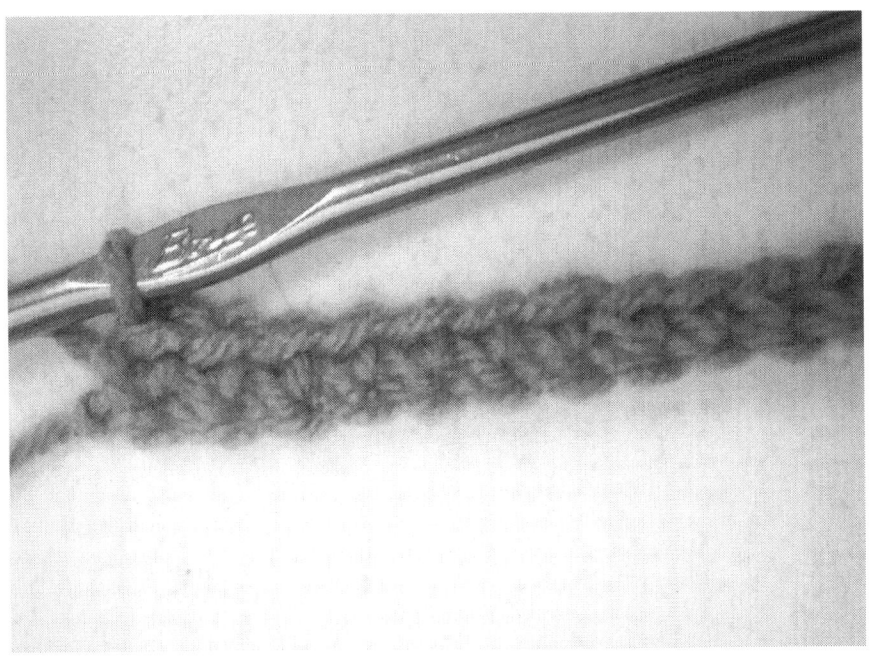

Completed row of single crochet

Double Crochet

Double crochet stitches are the base for many other types of stitches. If you are crocheting your first row as double crochet yarn over the hook and insert the hook into the fourth chain from the hook. (The first three chains count as the first double crochet stitch.) Yarn over again and pull the yarn through the chain stitch. You now have three loops on the hook. Yarn over and pull through the first two loops, yarn over one more time and pull through the last two loops on the hook.

To begin a new row of double crochet chain three and yarn over and insert the hook into the next stitch (not in the base of the chain three). Yarn over and pull through the stitch, yarn over and pull through the first two loops on the hook, yarn over and pull through the last two loops.

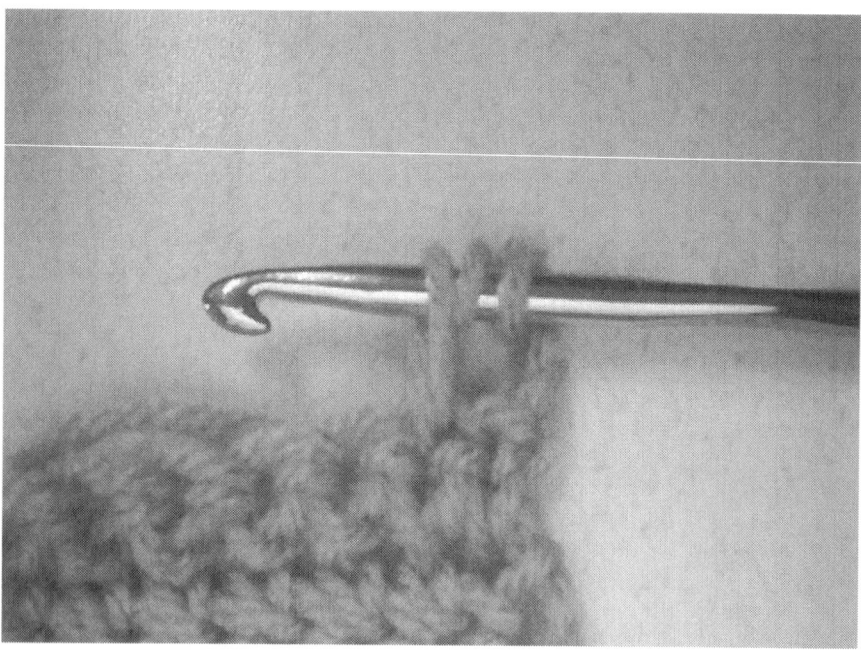

Yarn over and insert the hook into the next stitch, yarn over and pull through the stitch. You now have 3 loops on the hook.

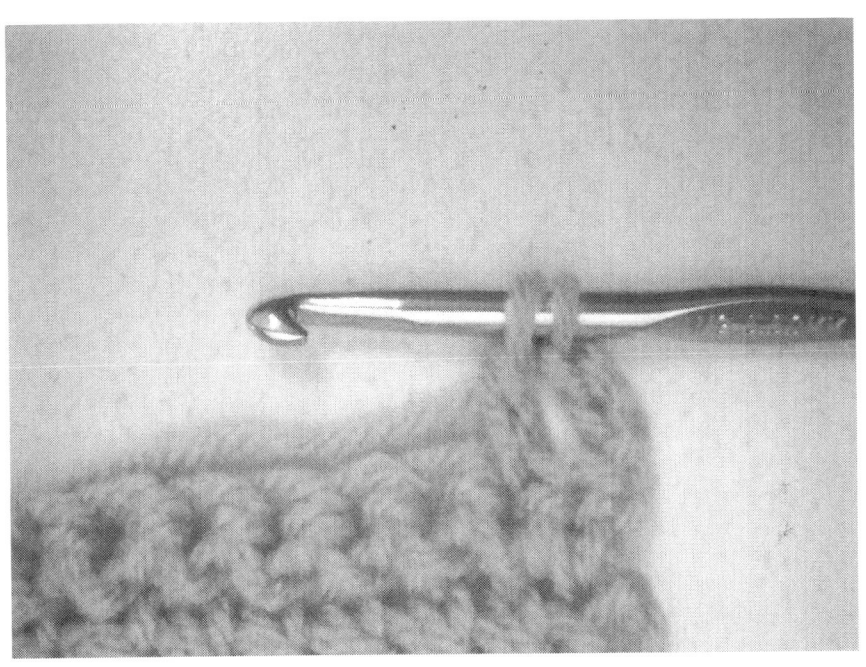

Yarn over and pull through the first 2 loops.

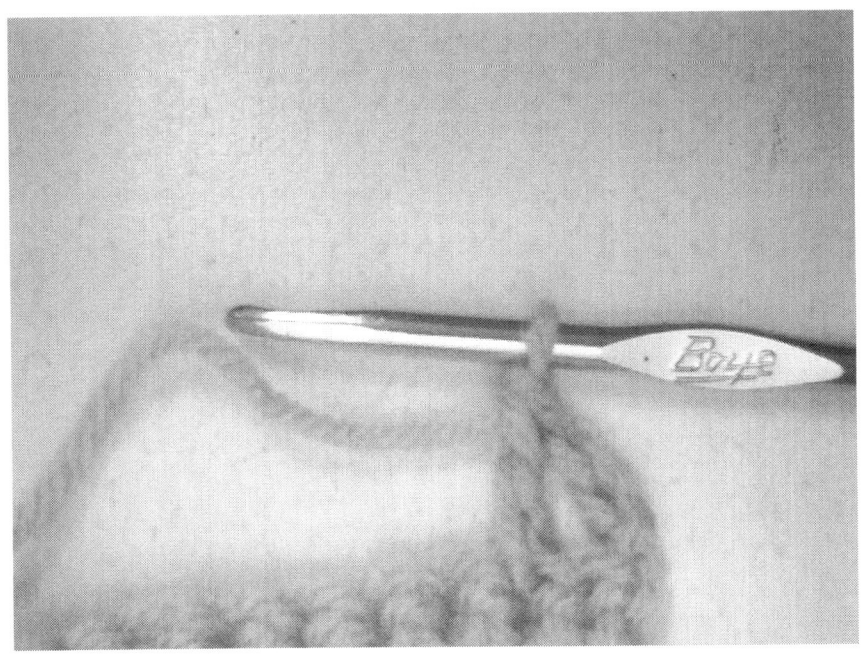

Yarn over and pull through the last 2 loops to complete the stitch.

Half Double Crochet

The half double crochet stitch is used a lot in hats. It is not as dense as the single crochet stitch, and not as high as the double crochet. If your first row is half double crochet yarn over and insert the hook into the third chain stitch from the hook (the first two chains count as the first half double in the row). Yarn over and pull the yarn through the chain stitch. You now have three loops on the hook. Yarn over and pull through all three loops at once. To begin a new row of half double crochet chain two. These count as the first stitch. Yarn over and insert the hook into the next stitch (not in the base of the chain two), yarn over and pull through the stitch, yarn over and pull through all three loops on the hook at once.

Treble Crochet

The treble, or triple, crochet stitch is a high lofty stitch which gives you a very loose fabric. It is generally used as part of more complex stitches such a shell stitches. If you are using treble crochet as your first row yarn over twice and insert the hook into the sixth chain from the hook (the first five chains are counted as the first stitch). Yarn over and pull through the chain stitch. You now have four loops on the hook. Yarn over and pull through the first two loops. Yarn over and pull through the next two loops, yarn over and pull through the last two loops. To begin a new row of treble crochet chain 5, yarn over twice and insert the hook into the next stitch (not into the base of the chain five). Yarn over and pull through the stitch. Yarn over and pull through the next two loops on the hook three times.

Yarn over twice, insert the hook into the next stitch, yarn over and pull through

Yarn over and pull through the first 2 loop, yarn over and pull through the next 2 loops, yarn over and pull through the last 2 loops.

Slip Stitch

The slip stitch is used to move the yarn to the correct position and to join rounds. Insert the hook into the next stitch, yarn over and pull the yarn through the stitch and the loop on the hook.

Decreases

Sometimes you need to decrease the number of stitches in a row or a round. This is accomplished by crocheting two stitches as one. You can do this will all stitches; single, half double, double, and treble. The abbreviations for these stitches are sc2tog, hdc2tog, dc2tog, and trb2tog. You may also crochet three stitches as one. This technique is used in ripple patterns. The abbreviations are sc3tog, hdc3tog, dc3tog, and trb3tog.

To crochet a dc2tog begin with a yarn over and insert the hook into the next stitch. Yarn over and pull through, yarn over and pull through the first two loops on the hook. Yarn over and insert the hook into the next stitch. Yarn over and pull through, yarn over and pull through the first two loops on the hook. Now you have three loops on the hook. Yarn over and pull through all three loops on the hook. You have now just crocheted two double crochet stitches as one and decreased the stitch count by one.

To crochet a sc3tog insert the hook into the next stitch, yarn over and pull through. Insert the hook into the next stitch, yarn over and pull through. Insert the hook into the next stitch, yarn over and pull through. You now have three loops on the hook. Yarn over and pull through all three loops at once. You have just crocheted three stitches as one and decreased the stitch count by two.

Double Crochet 2 Together (dc2tog)

Increases

Just as you may need to decrease the amount of stitches, you may also need to increase the number of stitches in a row or a round. This is very easy. Simply work more than one stitch into a single stitch. For example, if you're crocheting a hat from the crown to the brim you will need to shape the crown so that the hat fits correctly. The pattern will call for a number of single stitches and then a group of stitches to be worked into one stitch. Just work three single, half double, or double crochet stitches into one stitch.

Pattern Repeats

Designers use pattern repeats to help save space and make patterns easier to understand. Pattern repeats may be encased between asterisks, parentheses, or brackets. For example, if you come to an * in a pattern this is the beginning of a pattern repeat. Work the stitches until come to the next *. Go back to the first * and work to the next * again as many times as is called for in a pattern.

Here is an example:

Row 2: ch1, *3sc into the next st, ch3, sk 1 st* rep to end of row, sc into last st

In English this translates to chain one, begin a pattern repeat of three single crochet into the next stitch, chain three and skip one stitch. Now go back and work 3 single crochet into the next stitch, chain three and skip the next stitch until you reach the last stitch of the row and then work a single crochet into the last stitch.

Crochet Abbreviations	
Stitch Name	Abbreviation
Chain stitch	Ch
Stitch/Stitches	St/sts
Slip stitch	Sl st
Single crochet	Sc
Double crochet	Dc
Half double crochet	Hdc
Treble crochet	Trb
Repeat	Rep
Single crochet 2 together	Sc2tog
Double crochet 2 together	Dc2tog
Half double crochet 2 together	Hdc2tog

US Terms		UK Terms	
Chain	Ch	Chain	Ch
Slip stitch	Sl st	Slip stitch	Ss
Single crochet	Sc	Double crochet	Dc
Half double crochet	Hdc	Half treble	Htr
Double crochet	Dc	Treble	Tr
Treble crochet	Trb	Double treble	dtr

In this chapter we'll learn basic crochet techniques. It is important to develop good technique right off the bat, and I hope this chapter helps you do just that.

Even Edges

One of the biggest complaints I hear from beginners is that their edges aren't even. One side grows while the other one shrinks. The easiest way to prevent this is to count the stitches in each row as you work them. This way you have the correct number of stitches and your rows will be even.

Another way to ensure your edges are even is to end each row into the top of the turning chain of the previous row. For example, if you're working with single crochet then the last stitch is worked into the chain 1 of the turning chain of the previous row.

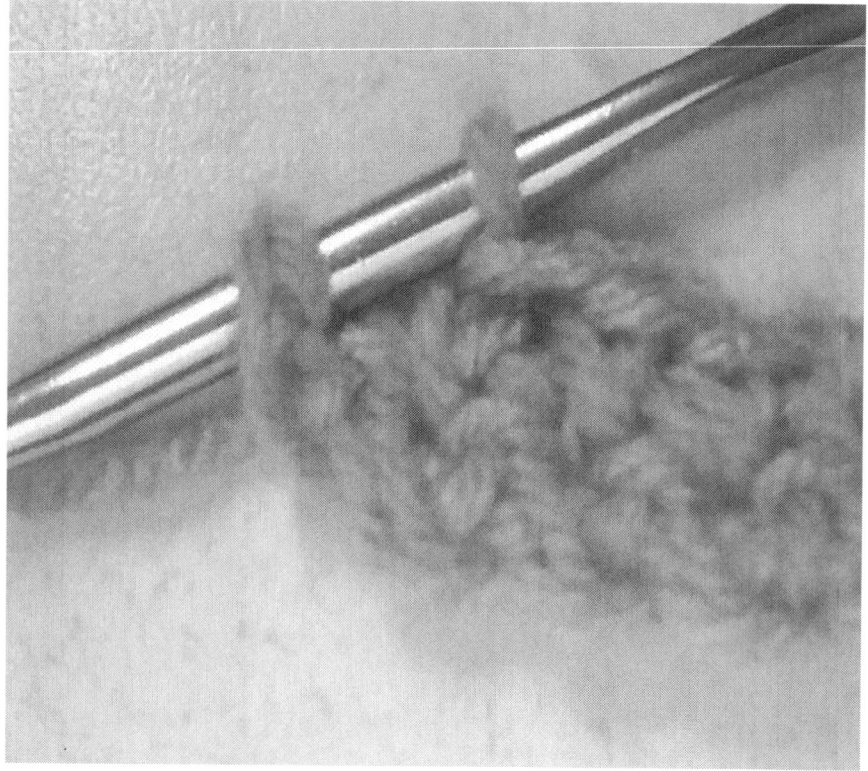

Always catch both loops of the chain stitch in the last stitch to secure the stitch and stabilize it. If you're working with double crochet then the last stitch of the row is worked into the third chain of the turning chain, and so on. When you begin a row always crochet the first stitch into the next stitch after the turning chain, not in the base of the turning chain.

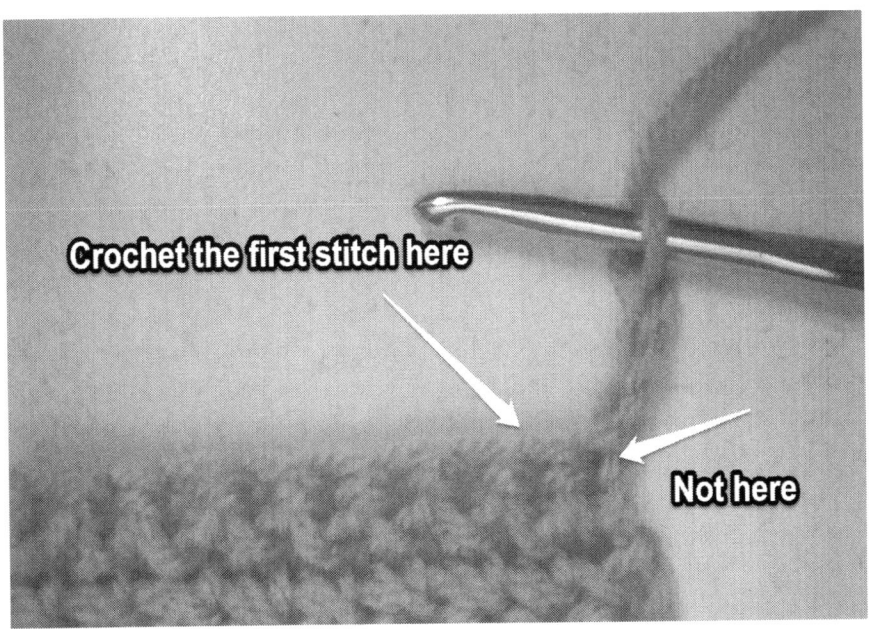

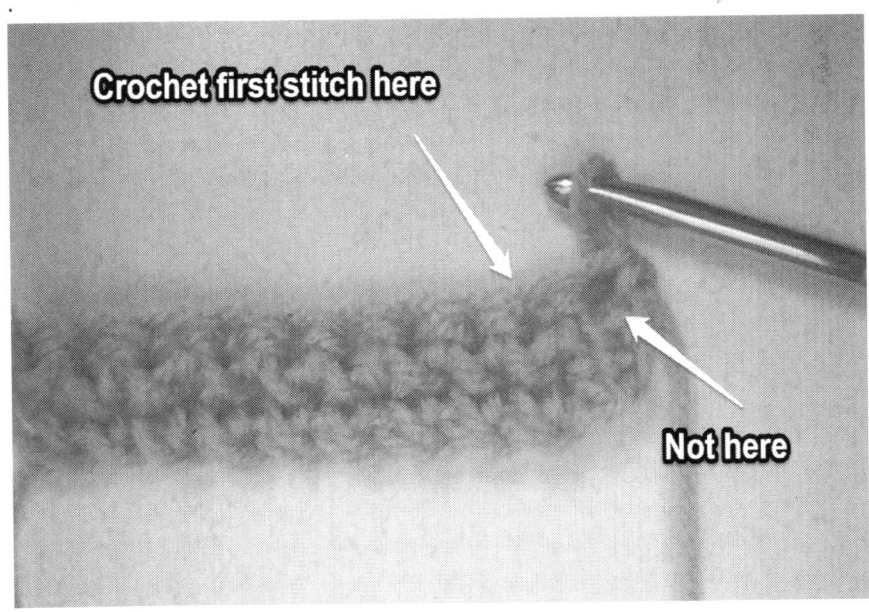

Crocheting in the Round

Hats, doilies, and other projects are crocheted in the round. Instead of working back in forth in rows, you work around and around. It is a good idea to place a clip on stitch marker in the first stitch of the round. This is especially important when you are using single crochet stitches since they are short and you may not be able to tell when you've reached the end of the round. When you reach the end of the round slip stitch into the last starting chain to join the round. Crochet the appropriate number of starting chain stitches to begin the next round.

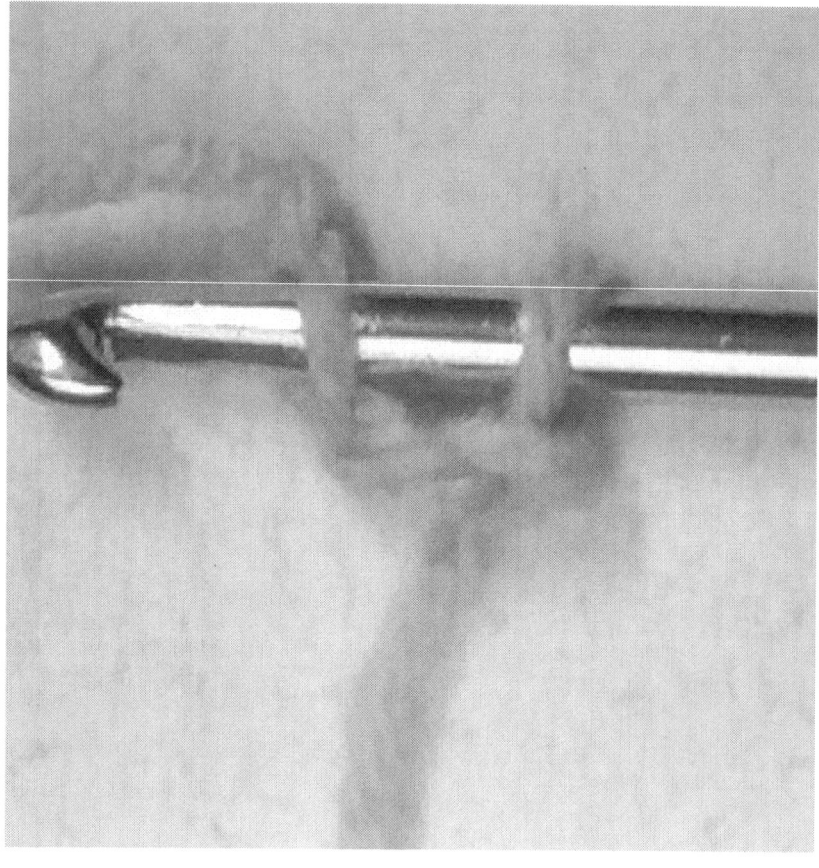

Slip stitch to join.

Invisible Join Method

Usually when you crochet in the round the joining seam is quite noticeable. It runs up the fabric diagonally because of the way the stitch counts end up and it perfectly normal. Instead of having a noticeable seam use the invisible join method to create a seam with is practically invisible. Work the correct number of stitch in the round. Work one more stitch in the same space as the starting chain. Instead of joining in the appropriate chain stitch, join in the next stitch. This hides the starting chain and since you worked one extra stitch, your stitch counts come out correctly.

Working with Color

I love color! I love to use lots of colors in my projects, I think color is one of the fun things about crochet and the yarn arts. Using color in crochet is very easy. If you are changing colors at the end of a row, simply work the last stitch until you have two loops on the hook. Grab the new color and pull it through the last two loops of the stitch. When you make your first chain stitch for the new row, catch the old color in the chain stitch to secure it. Crochet a few of the first stitches of the row in the new color and then go back and gently snug up both colors. Don't pull too tightly or it will make your stitches pucker.

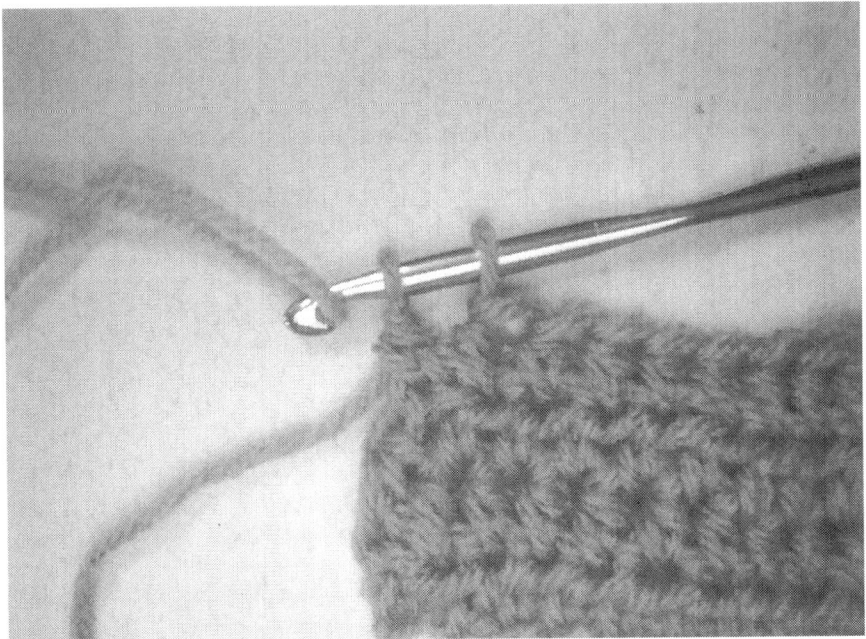

Pull the new color through the last 2 loops of the last stitch.

Now if you are going to be changing back to the old color after you come back across the row, don't fasten it off but leave it resting at the beginning of the row.

Then when you come back and are ready to change colors again simply pull it through the last two loops of the last stitch and repeat the process. This is known as carrying colors up the side of the fabric. Not only does this technique cut down on the number of tails you have to weave in, but it also secures the yarn.

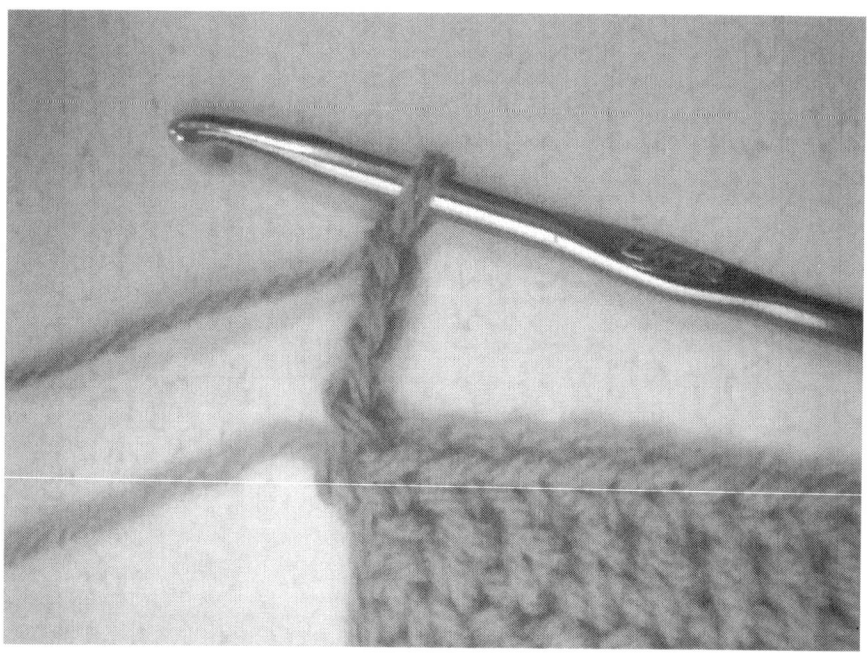

Catch the old color in the first chain stitch of the next row to secure it.

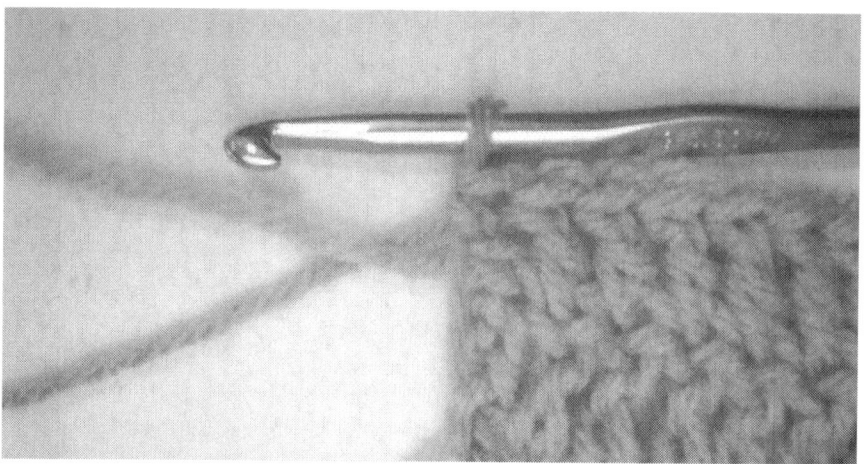

Colors carried up the fabric

Changing colors in a row is also very easy. You use the same method of pulling the new color through the last two loops of the last stitch of the old color. Catch the old color in the next stitch and then you can fasten the old color off leaving a long tail to weave in later.

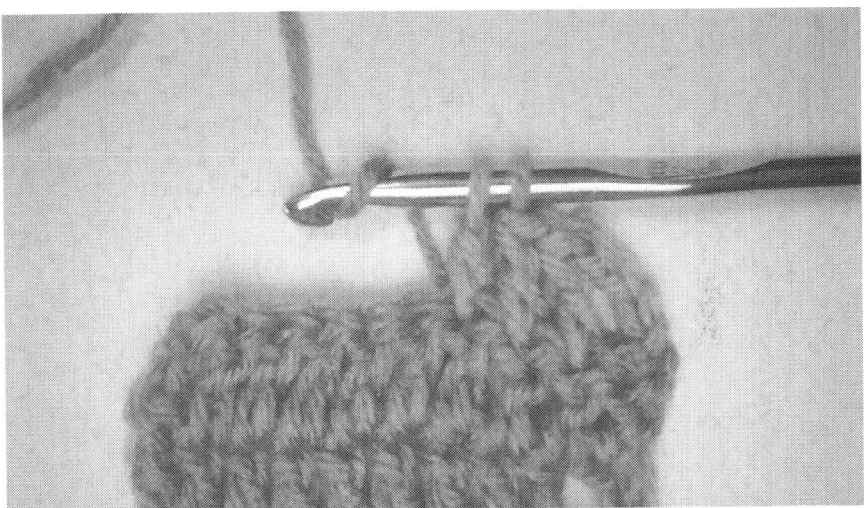

Pull the new color through the last 2 loops of the last stitch of the old color.

Completed color change mid-row

Weaving in Tails Securely

Knowing how to secure the tails of yarn you have from beginning and ending a project, and changing colors is important. You don't want to spend hours of hard work only to have your crochet stitches start to unravel and ruin a project.

I like to weave in the tails from changing colors as I go and not wait until the end of a project. But some folks wait until the end and weave in all of the tails at once, it's up to you how you do it.

Before you cut, or fasten off, the yarn leave at least six inches so you can weave it in. Thread a tapestry or blunt end needle with the tail. On the wrong side of the fabric weave the tail in and out of the stitches for about an inch. Turn the fabric and weave the tail in and out of the stitch for another inch going in a different direction. Turn the fabric and do this once more. Now you can fasten off the tail and it will be secure and stay put.

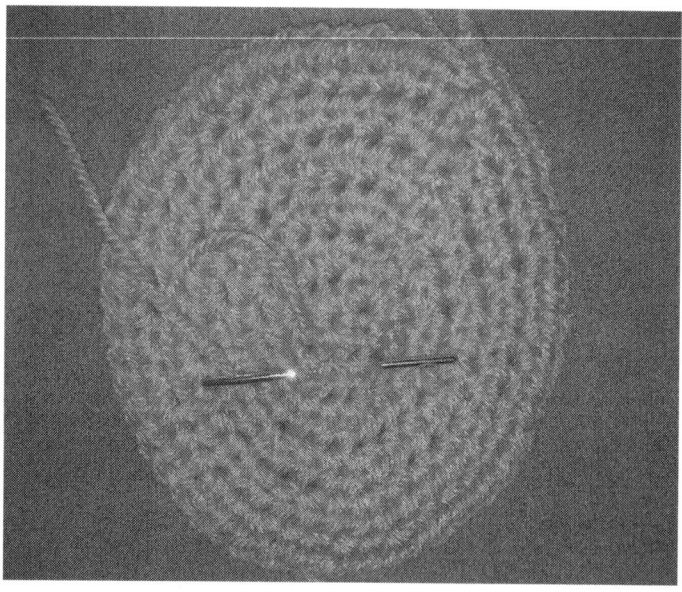

How to Create a Clean Edge for a Decorative Border

When you complete a project like an afghan and you want to add a decorative border crochet a round of single crochet around the edge to create a nice even border to work with. Work a single crochet stitch into each of the stitches on the top and bottom, work single crochet stitches as evenly as you can along the sides and crochet three single crochet stitches into each corner. This gives you a nice even and clean border to work with.

When you work along the edges you will have to estimate the number of stitches you will need and place them according to type of stitches were used in your project. For example, I find two single crochet stitches along the side of a double crochet works very well. You don't want to work too many stitches along the side or it will warp your fabric. Also you don't want to work too few or it will pull the fabric. It isn't an exact science and is really more of a "play it by ear" situation. Do what looks and feels the best, and don't worry about exact numbers along the sides.

Three stitches are worked in the corners so that you get a nice sharp corner. When you go around the corner again work the next three stitches into the middle stitch of the corner. This keeps your corners sharp and in the correct place.

In this chapter we'll learn some fun stitches you can use to create texture and interest in your projects. These stitches are just variations of the basic crochet stitches and can be learned very easily by beginners.

Shell Stitch

The shell stitch is a very versatile and useful stitch. All a shell stitch consists of are groups of double or half double crochet stitches worked all in one stitch. Granny Squares use three double crochet stitches in one stitch to form the iconic shells that they are known for. Shell stitches also make a sweet border on many projects.

In the image below there are three double crochet stitches worked into one stitch. One stitch is skipped and a single crochet stitch is then worked in the next stitch. Skip the next stitch and work three double crochet stitches into the next stitch. If this were written out in a pattern it would look like this:

3dc into the next st, sk 1 st, sc into the next st, sk 1 st, 3dc into the next st

Or it may look like this *3dc, sk1 st, sc, sk 1 st* The asterisks denote pattern repeats. Begin at the first asterisk and work the stitches to the next asterisk. Go back to the first one and repeat the pattern as many times as the pattern says.

Always check and see how many stitches are used in a shell for the pattern. Some patterns call for three or five while others may call for as many as 9 or 10.

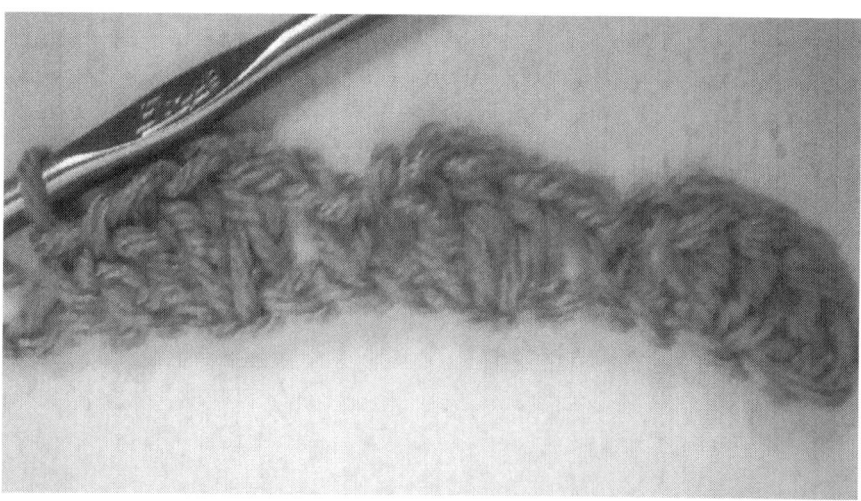

Cluster Stitch

The cluster stitch is a very pretty stitch. It has a bit of a different texture than a shell stitch. Cluster stitches generally contain three or four double crochet stitches. For a three double crochet cluster stitch begin with a yarn over and insert the hook into the next stitch. Yarn over and pull through the stitch, yarn over and pull through the first two loops of the hook. Yarn over and insert the hook into the same stitch, yarn over and pull through, yarn over and pull through the first two loops on the hook. You now have three loops on the hook. Yarn over and insert the hook into the same stitch again, yarn over and pull through, yarn over and pull through the first two loops on the hook. Now you have four loops on the hook. Yarn over and pull through all four loops at once. This forms the "eye" of the hook. Chain one to lock the stitch.

Row of cluster stitches

Bobble or Puff Stitch

The bobble or puff stitch gets its name from the fact the stitch puffs out from the fabric. Yarn over and insert the hook into the next stitch, yarn over and pull through. Repeat this process three more times. You will now have nine loops on the hook. Yarn over and pull through all nine loops at once. Chain once to lock the stitch. Single crochet into the next stitch. The puff stitch will puff out on the wrong side of the fabric. You can pop it onto the right side, or leave it.

Yarn over and pull through four times (9 loops on the hook)

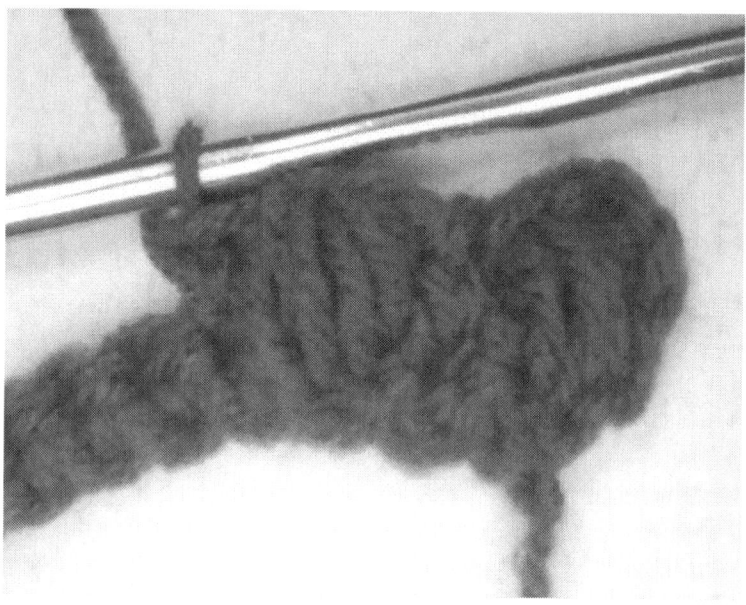

Completed puff stitches

Long or Spike Double Crochet Stitch

The spike stitch is a very decorative stitch which adds a lot of interest and texture to your projects. It is crocheted like a double crochet stitch except you drop down to the previous row or two rows below to insert the hook. To begin yarn over and insert the hook into the stitch in the previous row. Yarn over and pull through the stitch, draw the yarn up level with the active row, yarn over and pull through the first two loops on the hook. Yarn over and pull through the last two loops on the hook.

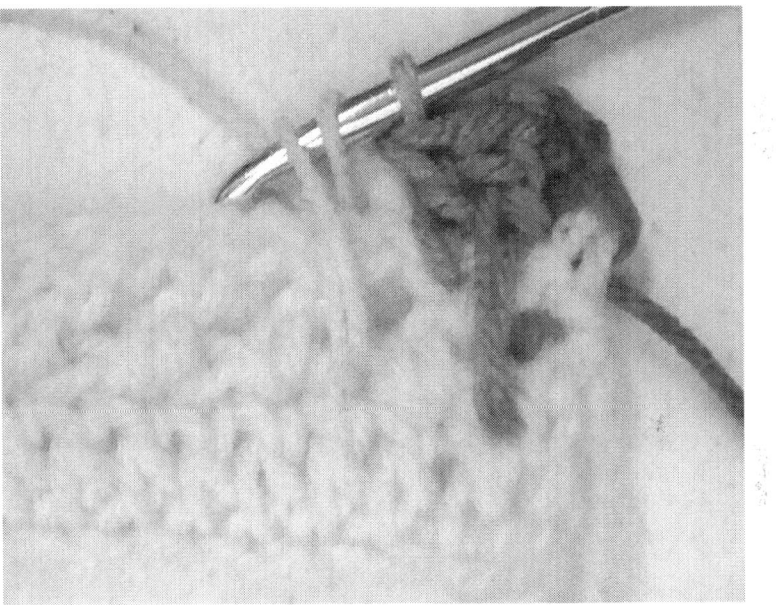

Insert the hook into the stitch in the row below

Crab or Reverse Single Crochet Stitch

The crab or reverse single crochet stitch is a decorative finishing stitch. It gives an edge a very interesting and attractive texture. Instead of working from right to left, you will be working from left to right (for right handed crocheters). Insert the hook into the stitch to the right, yarn over and pull through both loops on the hook. Continue to work left to right and join in the chain one of the beginning of the row or round.

Crab Stitch

Back Loop and Front Loops Stitches

If you look at the top of a crochet stitch you will see there are two loops which form a V. Normally you would insert the hook under both of these loops, but with a back or front loops stitch you only use one of these loops. For a back loop stitch insert the hook into the back loop, not under both loops. For a front loops stitch, insert the hook under the front loop of the stitch.

Back loop stitches create a subtle horizontal line on the right side of the fabric. Front loop stitches create this line on the wrong side of the fabric.

Back loop double crochet (blodc)

Front Loop Double Crochet (flodc)

Back and Front Post Stitches

If we look again at a crochet stitch, we will see that there is a post for each stitch. It is around this post that back or front post stitches are crocheted. To crochet a back post double crochet stitch yarn over and insert the hook from the back to the front around the post. Yarn over and draw the yarn around the post and finish the stitches as normal.

A front post double crochet is worked by yarning over and inserting the hook from the front the back around the post. Yarn over and draw the yarn around the post and then finish the stitches as normal.

Back post stitches create a raised horizontal ridge on the right side of the fabric. Front post stitches create a vertical ridge on the right side of the fabric. Back and front post stitches are used to create crochet cables and other decorative effects in patterns.

Yarn over and insert the hook from the back to the front around the post.

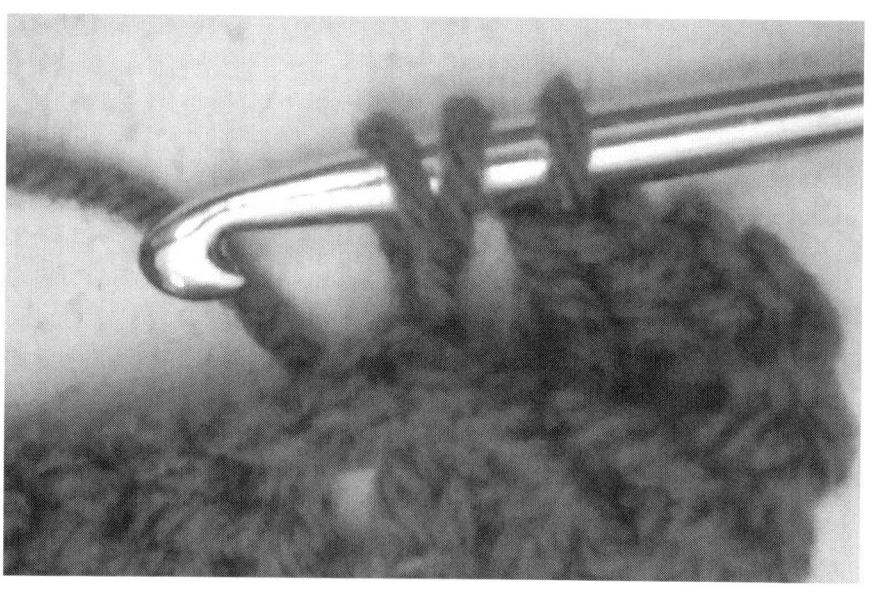

Yarn over and pull the yarn around the post.

Yarn over and insert the hook from the front to the back for a front post double crochet stitch.

Front post stitches

Back post stitches

This chapter contains some of my favorite patterns I have designed for the beginner. These patterns can be worked with the stitches and techniques I taught you in this book. I hope you enjoy working them and making them your own.

Please feel free to sell any items you may make with these patterns, but if you would like to share a pattern please share the link to this book on Amazon.

Striped Cotton Dishcloth

Dishcloths are some of my favorite projects. They work up fast and make great gifts. They are also much thicker and larger than store bought versions.

Materials Needed

1 skein each of Premier Home cotton/polyester yarn in Lime Green (Color A) and Poolside (Color B). You will also need a size I/9 (5.50mm) crochet hook and a tapestry needle.

Gauge: 13 double crochet and 10 rows in pattern (dc and sc) equal 4 inch square

Dishcloth measures 9 ½ inches tall and 10 inches wide.

Notes: Change colors by pulling the new color through the last 2 loops of the last stitch of the row. Don't fasten off the yarn after you change color, carry it up the side of the dishcloth by catching it under the first chain stitch of the new row.

With Color A chain 28

Row 1: dc into the 4th ch from the hook, dc across row, turn (26 stitches)

Row 2: ch3, dc across row, turn

Row 3: ch1, sc across row, turn

Rows 4 & 5: Repeat Rows 2 & 3 with Color B

Rows 6 & 7: Repeat Rows 2 & 3 with Color A

Rows 8-17: Repeat Rows 4-7, fasten off Color B after Row 15

Row 18: ch3, dc across, fasten off Color A, weave in the tails with a tapestry needle before working edging

Edging:

Round 1: Join Color B in any corner, ch1, 2 sc into the same space, sc across the top, 3sc into the corner, sc evenly along the side, 3sc into corner, sc across the bottom, 3sc into the corner, and sc evenly along the side, join in ch1

Round 2: ch1, 3 sc into next st, sc into each st working 3sc into each corner, join in ch1, fasten off and weave in tails

Ripple Washcloth or Placemat

You can use the colors that match your décor, and use acrylic or cotton medium weight yarn.

Materials Needed

Three colors of cotton or any medium weight yarn. I used Premier Home in Turquoise (Color A), Off White (Color B), and Water Lilies (Color C). You will also need a size US J/10 (6.00mm) crochet hook and a tapestry needle.

With Color A crochet 35 fdc

Row 1: ch3, 2dc into 1ˢᵗ st, dc into each of the next 4 sts, dc3tog twice, dc into each of the next 6 sts, 3dc into the next st twice, dc into each of the next 4 sts, 3dc into the last st, turn

Row 2 & 3: Repeat Row 1

Rows 4-6: With Color B Repeat Row 1

Rows 7-9: With Color C Repeat Row 1

Rows 10-12: With Color B Repeat Row 1

Rows 13-15: With Color A Repeat Row 1, do not fasten off

Edging: ch1, sc across the top of the placemat, 3sc into corner, sc evenly across side, 3sc into corner, sc across the bottom of the placemat, 3sc into corner, sc across side ending with 2sc into corner, join in chain 1.

Shell Stitch Earwarmer

This pattern is written for 6 months, but refer to the table in the Reference section of this book for a chart on head sizes to adjust the size to fit your needs.

Materials Needed

1 skein of Red Heart Super Saver in Blue (Color A). You won't need an entire skein and one skein will make several headbands. You will also need a size US I/9 (5.50mm) crochet hook, and a tapestry needle.

Gauge: 24 stitches and 7 rows of shells equals 4 inch square

Earwarmer measures about 16 inches long and about 3 ½ inches wide when completed.

Chain 10

Row 1: sc into the 3th ch from the hook, dc across row, turn (9 sts)

Row 2: ch3 *sk 1 st, 3dc into next st* rep twice, sk1 st, dc, turn

Row 3: ch3, sk 1 st, 3dc into the next st *sk 2 sts, 3dc into the next st* repeat once, sk 2 st, dc into 3rd ch, turn (shells are worked into the 2nd dc of the shell in the previous row)

Rows 4-21: Repeat Row 3

Row 22: ch1, sc across row, fasten off and leave a long tail

Hold the two ends of the earwarmer together and use a whip stitch to sew them together. Catch only the outside loops of the end stitches in the whip stitch to form an almost invisible seam. Fasten off and weave in tails.

Darling Daughter Slouchy Beanie

The self-striping yarn makes this beanie look like it is much harder to crochet than it really is. Pattern is sized for an adult.

Materials Needed

1 skein Mary Maxim Prism yarn in the color Autumn Mist. This is a weight 3 yarn and what is called a long strand variegated yarn. This means the color changes are gradual and make very pretty stripes in the hat. You will also need a size G/8 (5.00mm) crochet hook and a tapestry needle to weave in the tails.

Gauge: 7 cluster stitches and 6 rows in pattern equals 4 inch square

Hat measures 13 inches long and 16 inches in circumference at the brim when finished.

Notes: This hat is sized for an adult. If you would like to crochet it for a child omit Round 6.

The hat is crocheted from the crown down to the brim. You can make the hat longer or shorter to taste, simply increase the amount of rounds of the main pattern.

Chain 4, join to form a ring

Round 1: ch3, 9 dc into ring (work stitches around the ring, not into the chain stitches), join in the 3rd ch

Round 2: ch3, dc into the same st, work 2 dc into each st around, join in 3rd ch

Round 3: ch3, dc into the same st *dc into the next st, 2dc into the next st* repeat around, join in 3rd ch

Round 4: ch3, dc into same st *dc into each of the next 2 sts, 2dc into the next st* repeat around, join in 3rd ch

Round 5: ch3, dc into same st *dc into each of the next 3 sts, 2dc into the next st* repeat around, join in 3rd ch

Round 6: ch3, dc into same st *dc into each of the next 4 sts, 2dc into the next st* repeat around, join in 3rd ch

Round 7: ch4, sk 1 st, dc into next st, ch1 *dc into the next st, ch1, sk 1 st* repeat around, join in 3rd ch

Round 8: sl st into ch1 sp, ch3, 3dc cluster st in same ch1 sp, work a 4dc cluster st in each ch1 sp, join in 3rd ch

Round 9: sl st into space between the 1st and 2nd cluster stitches, ch4, *dc into the space between the next 2 cluster stitches, ch1* repeat around, join in the 3rd ch

Rounds 10-18: Repeat Rounds 8 & 9

Round 11: Repeat Round 9

Round 12: ch1, sc in each st around, join in ch1

Round 13: ch1, sc in each of the next 5 sts, sc2tog *sc in each of the next 6 sts, sc2tog* repeat around, join in ch1

Round 14: ch2, hdc in each st around join in 2nd ch

Round 15: ch2, hdc in each of the next 5 sts, hdc2tog *hdc into each of the next 6 sts, hdc2tog* repeat around

Round 16 & 17: Repeat Round 14, fasten off after Round 17. Thread a tapestry needle with the tails and weave them in securely.

Chunky Slouchy Beanie

I used a nice chunky yarn to crochet this warm beanie. The pattern uses front post double crochet (fpdc) stitches to create vertical ridges in the hat.

Materials Needed

You will need a weight 5 yarn. I used Premier Deborah Norville Serenity in the color Majesty. You will also need a size K/10 1/2 (6.50mm) crochet hook, and a tapestry needle.

Beanie measures around 9 inches long and 23 inches in circumference when completed.

Chain 4, join to create a ring

Round 1: ch3, 15dc into the ring, join in 3rd ch

Round 2: ch3, 2dc into each st around, end with a dc into the base of ch3, join in 3rd ch (use this join method for each round)

Round 3: ch3 *fpdc around the next st, 2dc into the next st* rep around, join

Round 4: ch3 *fpdc around the next st, dc into the next st, 2dc into the next st* rep around, join (the fpdc stitches should line up)

Rounds 5-8: ch3 *dc into each of the next 3 sts, fpdc around the next st* rep around, join (work around and skip the chain 3, join in the fpdc to create an invisible seam)

Round 9: ch1, sc into each st around, join in ch1

Rounds 10-12: ch1 *sc into each of the next 6 sts, sc2tog* rep around, join in ch1

Round 13: ch1, sc into each st around, join in ch1, fasten off and weave in ends.

How to Crochet a Granny Square

Granny squares are crocheted in the round. First chain 4 and join with a slip stitch in the first chain to form a ring. The first round of stitches is not crocheted into the 4 chain stitches, but into the center of the ring.

Chain 3 and crochet 2 double crochet. The chain 3 counts as the first double crochet. Chain 1 and then crochet 3 more double crochet. Chain 1 and crochet 3 more double crochet twice more. Join with a slip stitch into the 3rd chain of the starting chain (the first chain 3).

Round 1

If you are changing colors for the next round cut the yarn and leave a long tail to weave in later. Make a slip knot and place it on your hook. Insert the hook into a chain 3 space and join the new color with a slip knot.

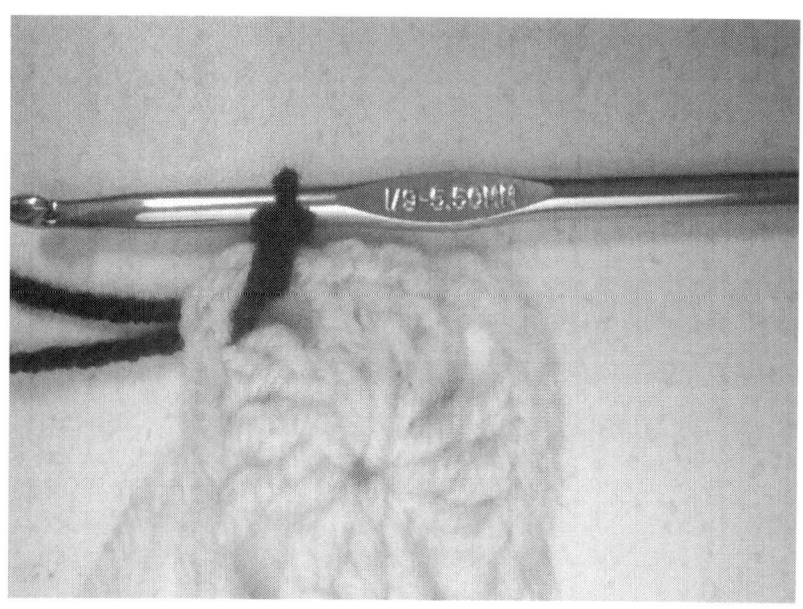

Joining a new color

If you are not changing colors slip stitch to the next chain 3 space. This will position your yarn in the correct space to begin the next round. Chain 3, crochet 2 more double crochet and chain 3. Crochet 3 more double crochet into the same chain 3 space. This is the first corner. Chain 1, into the next chain 3 space work 3 double crochet, chain 3, and 3 double crochet. Chain 1 and into the next chain 3 space work 3 double crochet, chain 3, and 3 double crochet. Repeat this again in the last chain 3 space, chain 1 and join with a slip stitch into the 3rd chain of the starting chain. You should have four sets of 3 double crochet, chain 3, 3 double crochet separated by a chain 1.

Round 2

To begin the third round either join a new color or slip stitch to the next chain 3 space. Chain 3 and crochet 2 double crochet, chain 3, and 2 double crochet into the first chain 3 space. Chain 1 and work 3 double crochet chain 1 into the next chain1 space. Work around the square crocheting 3 double crochet, chain 3, 3 double crochet, chain 1 into each chain 3 space (corners), and 3 double crochet, chain 1 into each chain 1 space.

3 round Granny square

You can make your squares as large or as small as you like. Just keep fastening off the yarn and joining a new color into a chain 3 space, or slip stitch to the first chain 3 space to begin a new round. If you want your square to be perfectly straight, turn the square after each round and do not slip stitch to the next chain 3 space. This will prevent the natural lean that occurs in the middle of larger Granny squares. If you're only going to make your squares three or four rounds big, you won't really have to worry about the lean. It usually occurs in larger squares.

Granny Square Potholder

This is a double thick potholder ready for the hottest pots and pans. The solid Granny Square provides a base and protection for your surfaces.

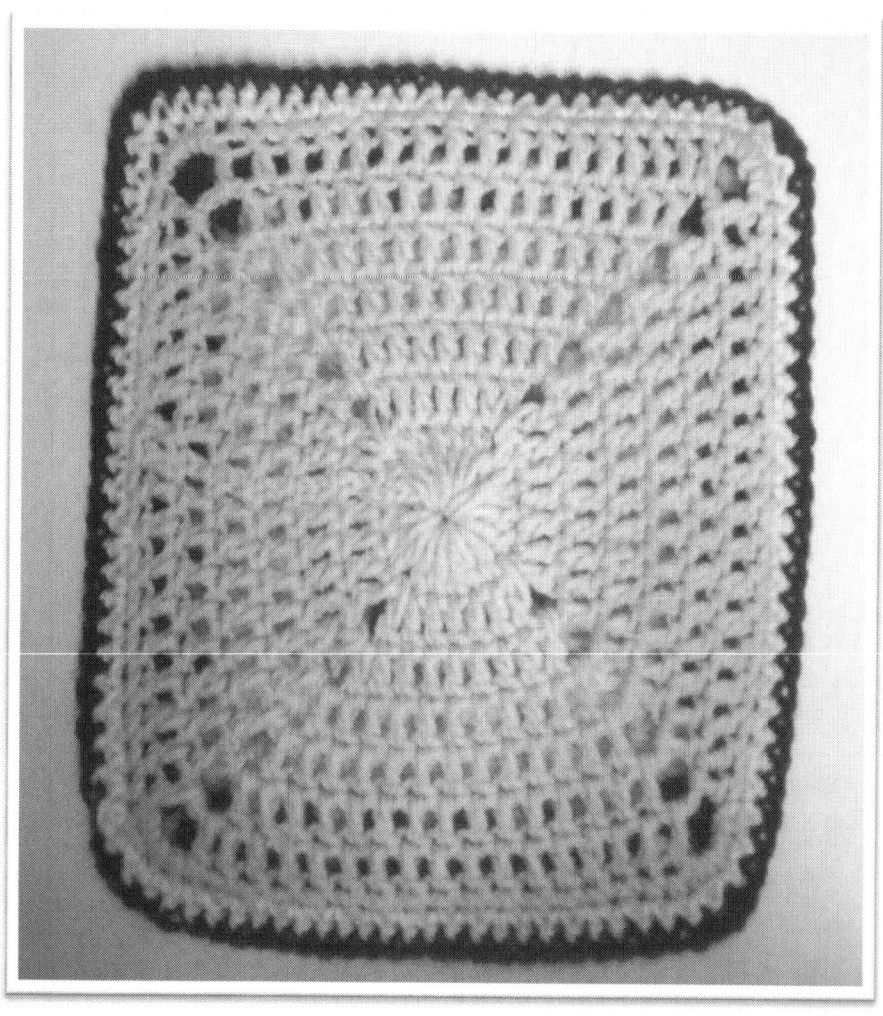

Materials Needed

Four colors of medium weight yarn. I used Red Heart Super Saver in Soft Navy (Color A), Blue (Color B), Light Blue (Color C), and Soft White (Color D). You will also need a size US I/9 (5.50mm) and a tapestry needle.

Granny Square

With Color A ch4 join in 1st chain to for a ring

Round 1: ch3, 2dc into ring *ch3, 3dc into ring* rep three times, join in 3rd ch, fasten off

Round 2: join Color B into a ch3 sp, ch3, 2dc into same ch3 sp, ch3, 3dc into same ch3 sp *ch1, into next ch3 sp work (3dc, ch3, 3dc)* rep around three times, join in 3rd ch, fasten off

Round 3: Join Color C in a ch3 sp, ch3, 2dc, ch3, 3dc into the same ch3 sp, ch1 *ch3 in the next ch1 sp, ch1, (3dc, ch3, 3dc) into the next ch3 sp, ch1*) rep around and join in 3rd ch, fasten off

Round 4: Join Color D in a ch3 sp, ch3, 2dc, ch3, 3dc into the same ch3 sp, ch1 *3dc into the next ch1 sp, ch1, 3dc into the next ch1 sp, ch1, (3dc, ch3, 3dc) into the next ch3 sp, ch1* rep around, join in 3rd ch, fasten off

Round 5: Join Color C in a ch3 sp, ch3, 2dc, ch3, 3dc into the same ch3 sp, ch1 *work 3dc, ch1 into each ch1 sp, (3dc, ch3, 3dc) into each ch3 sp, ch1* rep around, join in 3rd ch, fasten off

Round 6: Join Color A in a ch3 sp, ch3, 2dc, ch3, 3dc into the same ch3 sp, ch1 *work 3dc, ch1 into each ch1 sp, (3dc, ch3, 3dc) into each ch3 sp, ch1* rep around, join in 3rd ch

Round 7: ch1, sc into each st working 3sc into each corner (ch3) sp around, join in ch1, fasten off. Weave in all tails.

Solid Granny Square

With Color C ch4 join in 1st ch to form ring

Round 1: ch3, 4dc into ring, ch1 *5dc into ring ch1* rep around three times, join in 3rd ch

Round 2: ch3, dc into each of the next 4 sts, ch3 *dc into each of the next 7 sts, ch3* rep around three times, dc into each of the next 2 sts, join in 3rd ch

Round 3: ch3, dc into each of the next 5 sts, ch3 *dc into each of the next 9 sts, ch3* rep around three times, dc into each of the next 3 sts, join in 3rd ch

Round 4: ch3, dc into each of the next 6 sts, ch3 *dc into each of the next 11 sts, ch3* rep around three times, dc into each of the next 4 sts, join in 3rd ch

Round 5: ch3, dc into each of the next 7 sts, ch3 *dc into each of the next 13 sts, ch3* rep around three times, dc into each of the next 5 sts, join in 3rd ch

Round 6: ch3, dc into each of the next 8 sts, ch3 *dc into each of the next 15 sts, ch3* rep around three times, dc into each of the next 6 sts, join in 3rd ch

Round 7: ch3, dc into each of the next 9 sts, ch3 *dc into each of the next 17 sts, ch3* rep around three times, dc into each of the next 7 sts, join in 3rd ch,

Round 8: ch1, sc into each st working 5sc into each corner (ch3 sp), fasten off and weave in tails.

Joining

Hold wrong sides together and join Color D catching the loops of the stitches of both squares in the slip stitch. Ch1, sc in each st and work 5sc into each corner space catching the loops of both squares in each stitch. You will have to ease the stitches to make the sides match. To do this crochet 2 single crochets into the Granny Square motif but only crochet 1 stitch into the solid motif. You have to do this because the solid motif does not have as many stitches on the edge as the Granny Square.

Men's Watch Cap

This cap uses back loop only half double crochet to give it a bit of texture. It is sized for an adult.

Notes: Don't cut the yarn, but carry the color up the inside of the cap for a row. Use the invisible join method. Work the stitches across the round, work one more stitch into the base of the starting chain, and skip the chain 3 starting chain and join into the first stitch. This creates an almost invisible seam.

Materials Needed

You will need some medium weight yarn in two colors. I used Red Heart Super Saver in Soft Navy (Color A) and Soft White (Color B). You'll also need a size J/10 (6mm) crochet hook and a tapestry needle.

Hat measures about 8 inches in length and 24 inches in circumference when completed. The hat is sized for a large adult, but you can make it smaller by using a size I/9 for a regular adult size, or a size G/8 for a teen size hat.

With Color A chain 3, join to create ring

Round 1: ch2, 9hdc into ring

Round 1: ch2, 11hdc into the ring (insert the hook into the center of the ring, not into the chain stitches)

Round 2: ch2, hdc into same sp, h2dc into each chain st, join in 2nd ch

Round 3: ch2 *hdc into the next st, 2hdc into the next st* rep around, join in 2nd ch

Round 4: ch2 *hdc into each of the next 2 sts, 2hdc into the next st* rep around, join in 2nd ch

Round 5: ch2 *hdc into each of the next 3 sts, 2hdc into the next st* rep around, join in 2nd ch

Round 6: ch2 *hdc into each of the next 4 sts, 2hdc into the next st* rep around, join in 2nd ch

Rounds 7-10: ch2, blohdc (back loop only double crochet) in each st around, join in 2nd ch

Round 11: ch1, blosc in each st around, join in ch1

Round 12: ch1, sc in each st around, join in ch1

Round 13: With Color B ch1, sc in each st around, join in ch1

Round 14: With Color A ch1, sc in each st around, join in ch1, fasten off and weave in tails

Striped Cap

The pattern is sized for a child 6-12 years of age and measures about 6 inches long and 21 inches in circumference.

Notes: Carry the colors up the inside of the hat. Use the invisible join method to create a neat seam. Crochet the last stitch, and then one more stitch into the base of the chain two. Join in the stitch right after the beginning chain. The beginning chain will be hidden behind the first stitch, and the stitch count will be correct because of the extra stitch you worked into the base of the chain stitches.

Hat measures about 6 inches long and 21 inches in circumference when completed.

You will need two colors of medium weight yarn. I used Red Heart Super Saver in Aran (Color A) and Aruba Sea (Color B). You will also need a size I/9 (5.50mm) crochet hook, two small buttons, a sewing needle and thread, and a tapestry needle.

With Color A ch 3 and join to create a ring.

Round 1: ch2, 8hdc into the ring, join

Round 2: ch2, hdc into the same st, 2hdc into each st around, join

Round 3: With Color B ch2, hdc into the next st, 2hdc into the next st *hdc into the next 2 sts, 2hdc into the next st* rep around, join

Round 4: ch2, hdc into each of the next 2 sts, 2hdc into the next st *hdc into each of the next 3 sts, 2hdc into the next st* join

Round 5: With Color A ch2, hdc into each of the next 3 sts, 2hdc into the next st *hdc into each of the next 4 sts, 2hdc into the next st* join

Round 6: ch2, hdc in each st around, join

Rounds 7 & 8: With Color B repeat Round 6

Rounds 9 & 10: With Color A repeat Round 6

Rounds 11 & 12: With Color B repeat Round 6, fasten off after Row 12

Rounds 13 & 14: With Color A repeat Round 6, fasten off after Row 14

Brim

Attach Color B 15 stitches to the left of the back seam. (Make a slip knot and place it on the hook, insert the hook into the stitch and pull the yarn through the stitch and the slip knot to attach the yarn.) Place a stitch marker on the 16th stitch to the right of the back seam.

Row 1: ch1, sc to the stitch marker, turn

Row 2: ch2, hdc across, turn

Row 3: ch1, sc across, turn

Row 4: Repeat Row 2

Row 5: Repeat Row 3

At the end of Row 3 crochet down to the body of the hat and slip stitch into the first stitch. Turn the hat and crochet back up the side of the brim as evenly as you can, crochet 2 single crochet into the corner and single crochet across the last row. Crochet 3 single crochet into the corner and single crochet evenly down the side of the brim and join with a slip stitch into the last stitch. Fasten off and weave in tails.

Fold the brim up with the corners even with the second stripe. Sew a small button on each side of the hat at this point. What I did was split a strand of yarn and use it to sew on the buttons, but you can use sewing thread if you desire. Button up the brim and you're finished!

Chic City Clutch

This clutch bag is perfect for work or a night out. It is roomy enough to carry your essentials, but still gives you a chic sleek line.

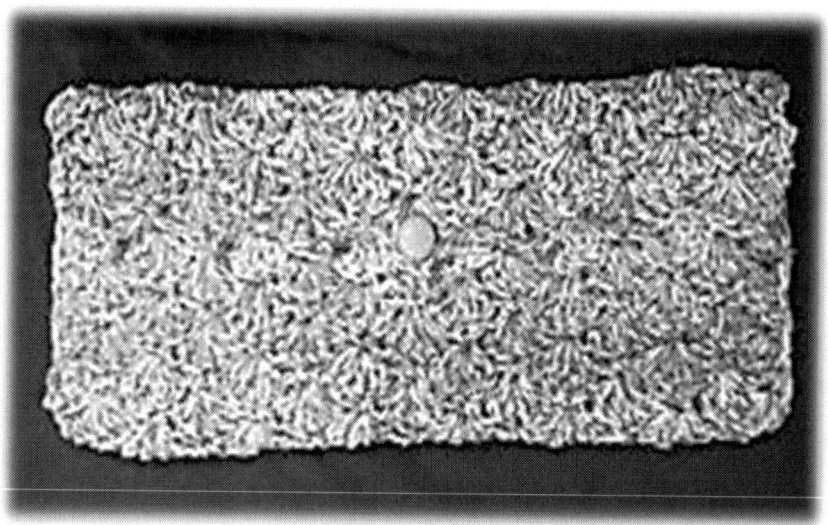

Materials Needed

You will need a ball of Premier Home yarn in Gray Splash, a size US G/6 (4.25mm) crochet hook, a tapestry needle, sewing needle and thread, and a small button.

Special Stitch

Picot Stitch – Chain 3, slip stitch into first chain

Chain 43

Row 1: dc into the 4th ch from the hook, dc across chain, turn

Row 2: ch3, 2dc into the 1stst (base of ch3) *sk2 sts, sc into next st, sk 2 sts, 5dc into next st* rep across, end with sk2 sts, sc into next st, 3dc into the top of the turning chain

Row 3: ch1 *5dc into next sc st, sc into the 3rd dc of the next shell* rep across ending with a sc into the top of the turning chain

Row 4: ch3, 2dc into sc *sc into the 3rd dc of the next shell, 5 dc into the next sc* rep across ending with 3dc into the top of the turning chain

Rows 5-24: Repeat Rows 3 & 4 (On Row 24 work a picot stitch on the 3rd dc of each shell cluster.) Weave in tails.

Assembly

Fold fabric with the foundation chain meeting the top of the 18th row. Beginning at the bottom right corner join yarn and ch1, single crochet evenly up the side, single crochet across the foundation chain and down the other side. Fasten off and weave in tails.

Sew a decorative button in the center of the front and use the third shell of the middle cluster as the button hole. You may wish to line the bag. If so simply cut a piece of decorative fabric to fit the inside, fold the raw edges under, and whip stitch it onto the stitches all of the way around the lining.

GLOSSARY OF CROCHET TERMS

I have included the majority of commonly used and standard crochet terms and abbreviations in this glossary for your reference. You may find special terms and abbreviations in patterns. These should be included in the key or the notes provided by the designer.

[ ] = work instructions within brackets as many times as directed

( ) = work instructions within parentheses as many times as directed

* = repeat the instructions following the single asterisk as directed

* * = repeat instructions between asterisks as many times as directed or repeat from a given set of instructions

approx = approximately

beg = begin(s)(ning)

bet = between

bo = bobble stitch

bpdc = Back Post double crochet

btwn = between

CC = contrasting color

ch(s) = chain(s)

ch-space = space previously made

cl = cluster stitch

cont = continu(e)(s)(ing)

dbl = double

dc = double crochet

dec = decreas(e)(s)(ing)

dtr = double treble (triple) crochet

est = establish(ed)

ext = extension

foll = follow(s)(ing)

fpdc = front post double crochet

fpsc = front post single crochet

fptr = front post triple crochet

frog = rip out or undo stitches

g = gram

hdc = half double crochet

hoth = hot off the hook

inc = increas(e)(s)(ing)

lp st = loop stitch

lp(s) = loop(s)

m = meters

MC = main color

meas = measure(s)

mm - millimeters

opp = opposite

oz = ounces

pat = pattern

pc = popcorn

Pm = place marker

rem = remain(s)(ing)

rep = repeat(s)(ing)

rf = right front

RH = right hand

rnd(s) = round(s)

RS = right side

rsc = reverse single crochet

sc = single crochet

sc2tog = single crochet 2 together

sc3tog = single crochet 3 together

sk = skip

sl = slip

sl st = slip stitch

sm = slip marker

sp(s) = space(s)

sq(s) = square(s)

st(s) = stitch(es)

t-ch = turning chain

tbl = through the back loop

tog = together

tr = treble (triple) crochet

wip = work in progress

WS = wrong side

yo = yarn over

yoh = yarn over hook

yrh = yarn over (yarn round hook)

REFERENCE TABLES

This section contains handy tables you can use for reference.

Yarn Weight Chart			
Weight	Description	Recommended Hook	Stitches in 4"
0 Lace	Fingerling, Size 10 Crochet Thread	Steel 1.6-1.4mm/B-1	32-48
1 Superfine	Sock, Fingerling	2.25-3mm/B-1 to E-4	21-32
2 Fine	Sport, Baby	3.4-4.5mm/E-4 to 7	16-20
3 Light	DK, Light Worsted	4.5-5.5mm/7 to I/9	12-17
4 Medium	Worsted, Afghan, Aran	5.5-6.5mm/I-9 to K-10 ½	11-14
5 Bulky	Chunky, Craft, Rug	6.5-9mm/K-10 ½ to M-13	8-11
6 Super Bulky	Super Bulky, Roving	9-15mm/m-13 to Q	7-9
7 Jumbo	Jumbo, Roving	15mm and up	6 or less

Crochet Abbreviations	
Stitch Name	Abbreviation
Chain stitch	Ch
Stitch/Stitches	St/sts
Slip stitch	Sl st
Single crochet	Sc
Double crochet	Dc
Half double crochet	Hdc
Treble crochet	Trb
Repeat	Rep

Single crochet 2 together	Sc2tog
Double crochet 2 together	Dc2tog
Half double crochet 2 together	Hdc2tog

US Terms		UK Terms	
Chain	Ch	Chain	Ch
Slip stitch	Sl st	Slip stitch	Ss
Single crochet	Sc	Double crochet	Dc
Half double crochet	Hdc	Half treble	Htr
Double crochet	Dc	Treble	Tr
Treble crochet	Trb	Double treble	dtr

US Hook Sizes			
US Size	Millimeter Size	US Size	Millimeter Size
B/1	2.25mm	J/10	6mm
C/2	2.75mm	K/10 ½	6.5mm
D/3	3.25mm	L/11	8mm
E/4	3.5mm	M-N/13	9mm
F/5	3.75mm	N-P/15	10mm
G/6	4mm	P/Q	15mm
7	4.5mm	Q	16mm
H/8	5mm	S	19mm
I/9	5.5mm		

US Sizes	Metric Sizes	UK/Canadian
0	2.0	14
1	2.25	13
2	2.75	12
-	3.0	11
3	3.25	10
4	3.50	-
5	3.75	9
6	4.0	8
7	4.5	7
8	5.0	6
9	5.5	5
10	6.0	4
10 ½	6.5	3
-	7.0	2
-	7.5	1

11	8.0	0
13	9.0	00
15	10.0	000
17	12.0	-
19	16.0	-
35	19.0	-

STEEL CROCHET HOOK CONVERSION

Metric (mm)	US	UK
3.5	00	-
3.25	0	0
2.75	1	1
2.25	2	1 1/2
2.1	3	2
2.0	4	2 1/2
1.9	5	3
1.8	6	3 1/2
1.65	7	4
1.5	8	4 1/2
1.4	9	5
1.3	10	5 1/2
1.1	11	6
1.0	12	6 1/2
.85	13	7
.75	14	-

Afghan and Throw Size Chart	
Size	**Measurements**
Crib	30 x 54 inches
Lapghan	36 x 48 inches
Twin Bed	48 x 78 inches
Long Twin Bed	48 x 84 inches
Double Bed	60 x 78 inches
Queen Size Bed	66 x 84 inches
King Size Bed	80 x 84 inches

Hat Measurement Guide			
	Circumference	**Diameter**	**Ear to Crown**
Newborn	13.5	4.25	4.5
3 months	16	5	5.25
6 months	17	5.5	5.5
12 months	18	5.75	5.75
2 years	19	6	6
3-5 years	20	6.5	6.5

6-10 years	21	6.75	6.75
Adult Small	22	7	7
Adult Medium	23	7.5	7.5
Adult Large	24	7.75	7.75

LINKS TO WEBSITES AND VIDEOS ON CROCHET

In this section I have gathered together some of the links I have found very useful for anyone learning to crochet. I have also included links to the major yarn manufacturers. Many of them have free tutorials on crochet stitches and techniques. Be sure to check out the many page devoted to crochet on Facebook, and the hundreds of board on Pinterest. These links are just the tip of the iceberg, and I'm sure you'll find your favorites as you explore online.

The Craft Yarn Council

http://craftyarncouncil.com

The Craft Yarn Council is the industry's standard for crochet and knitting. On this site you will find practically everything you need to know about crochet and knitting. They offer free tutorials and guides for every facet of yarn and fiber art.

Red Heart

http://redheart.com

Red Heart offers hundreds of free patterns for all skill levels. They also carry a wide selection of yarn and tools for crochet and knitting.

Lion Brand

http://lionbrand.com

Lion Brand also offers hundreds of free patterns at every skill level. They have a wide selection of yarn and offer free tutorials for crochet and knitting on their website.

Yarnspirations

http://yarnspirations.com

This is the home for Caron, Paton, and Bernat yarn brands. You can find hundreds of free patterns for all sorts of projects at every skill level. They also have free tutorials and videos to help you learn and expand your crochet skills. They are the sponsors of another one of my favorite sites, The Crochet Crowd.

The Crochet Crowd

http://thecrochetcrowd.com

This is the mother load of free videos and tutorials. Mikey and the gang produce new videos, crochet alongs, and patterns on a regular basis. Be sure to sign up for their newsletter and free magazine, Mikey. Visit their YouTube channel and subscribe to keep up to date on their latest videos.

My Picot

http://mypicot.com

This designer creates some of the most beautiful stitches and work I've ever seen. Her patterns are free and you can download the PDF files to your computer to print out and work. She offers freebies from time to time and gives extensive tutorials for all of her patterns.

Zooty Owl

http://zootyowlcards.blogspot.com/

This is another very talented designer. She designed the popular Road Trip Scarf and regular updates her blog with new patterns and ideas.

Raverly

http://www.raverly.com

Okay, you must go to this site and set up an account. On it you can store pattern links, post pics of your latest projects, post pattern you have designed, and find thousands of patterns and ideas. Some patterns are free, while others are paid, but they are all posted by folks just like you and me who love crochet and want to share their skills and knowledge.

Craftsy

http://craftsy.com

If you want to learn a new skill, this is one of the best sites to visit. They have free classes and paid classes for all types of yarn and fiber arts. I've take classes on crochet cables, finishing techniques, and many other skills. The classes can be taken on your time and are very affordable. They also have yarn, tools, and notions at reasonable prices. Sometimes they run specials on yarn which are hard to pass up. (I once ordered 40 balls of Premier Home yarn when it was under $1.)

My Favorite YouTube Channels

These links will take you to YouTube channels which present crochet skills and projects in easy to understand steps and language. I like videos because you can start and stop them and work along with the host.

The Crochet Crowd YouTube Channel

https://www.youtube.com/channel/UCVbbBdiTKMCx5VIl4IKDU7A

Crochet Geek YouTube Channel

https://www.youtube.com/channel/UCOYP5XacoUw5ZFx8_X8IHVg

Crochet Ever After YouTube Channel

https://www.youtube.com/channel/UCjA1PYUIPYGRg7YXNDkrZBg

Crochet Kim YouTube Channel

https://www.youtube.com/channel/UCTFlxyBi1PWmlK5fjsdTYgg

Crochet Cabana YouTube Channel

https://www.youtube.com/channel/UCsXvtktGQhqOw-ppSBcGCzA

Naztazia YouTube Channel

https://www.youtube.com/channel/UCUCRKFasGHLgVo57NziOLJg

Expression Fiber Arts YouTube Channel

https://www.youtube.com/channel/UCDIIBzRhAFWF7ZCKo9MMIzA

Yarn Obsession YouTube Channel

https://www.youtube.com/channel/UCFYWUmnSgv4OBMdSIPrG45w
Learn How to Crochet 4 Granny Square Patterns

Learn How to Crochet and How to Crochet Granny Squares and
Three Variations Along with Joining Methods

By Florence Schultz

Table of Contents

INTRODUCTION

Who doesn't love Granny squares? The Granny square motif has been popular for many decades and for good reason. It gives you the chance to show your creativity through the use of color and placement of the squares, and it is a classic look. In this book you will learn about yarn and how to select the right yarn for your project, about crochet hooks, how to crochet basic stitches and techniques, how to crochet the basic Granny square and three Granny square variations. Next we finish up with three joining methods. With the skills you will learn in this book you will be on your way to a lifelong love of crochet and Granny squares.

Before we begin to learn how to crochet we first need to learn about yarn and hooks. Yarn comes in a wide variety of fibers, colors, and textures. In this chapter we'll learn about yarn, how to read a yarn label and choose the right yarn for your project, and we'll learn about crochet hooks and sizes.

Yarn Fibers

Yarn is produced from three main types of fibers; synthetic, animal, and plant. The manufacturing process is pretty standard for all three types. The fibers arrive at the manufacturing facility in bales which may be dyed at the facility or have been dyed before shipment. Next the fibers are cleaned and stretched into long strands resembling finished yarn. These strands are steamed, twisted, and wound up into balls and skeins. The difference between a ball and a skein is that a ball pulls the yarn from the outside, while a skein pulls the yarn from the center. Some yarn comes in hanks which are strands of yarn wrapped up into a long loose skein which must be wound up into a ball before use. If you try to use a hank without winding it up you will end up with a terrible tangled mess.

Synthetic Yarn

Synthetic yarn includes acrylic, polyester, microfiber, and other fibers used to create yarn. You are probably familiar with Red Heart Super Saver or Caron Soft yarn. These are examples of a synthetic yarn. Acrylic yarn of today comes in many colors and textures and is manufactured to be just as soft as wool and other natural fibers. Polyester, microfiber, and other synthetic fibers are used in blends to give the yarn stretch, durability, easy of care, and sheen.

Animal Fibers

The most commonly recognized animal fiber used for yarn is wool. Wool is taken from sheep and then combed, cleaned, and made into bales of wool fibers used to produce yarn. Wool gives you a springy warm crochet fabric and for many years was the choice for fiber artists. Alpaca is another popular choice for animal fiber based yarns. Alpaca is inexpensive and comes in many colors and textures. Silk is made from the cocoons of the silk worm. Silk is usually blended in with other fibers to create a very attractive yarn. Cashmere and angora are high end yarns. They can be a bit on the pricey side, but they are unmatched for softness and drape.

Plant Fibers

Plant fibers used to produce yarn include cotton, bamboo, linen, hemp, and soy. Cotton is the perfect choice for kitchen and bath items since it soaks up water and is very durable. Bamboo is nice for detailed projects like shawls or lace crochet. The stitch definition with bamboo is very pretty and the fabric is light and airy. Linen is made from the fibers of the flax plant. The fabric is light and suitable for summer and hot weather garments and accessories. Hemp and soy are natural choices for many projects and are a green alternative to other types of yarn.

Yarn Weight

Yarn comes in different weights. Each weight is suitable for a different type of project and hook size. Yarn ranges from lace and fingerling to heavy jumbo weights. When choosing a yarn for a pattern, pay close attention to the weight of yarn called for by the designer. You can substitute yarn brands, but not yarn weights. For example if the pattern calls for a fingerling weight yarn and you use medium weight yarn, your finished project will be much larger than the pattern. Always check the yarn label for the yarn weight and purchase the correct weight for the pattern.

The following table lists the different yarn weights and the recommended hook sizes for each weight.

Yarn Weight Chart			
Weight		**Description**	**Recommended Hook**	**Stitches in 4"**
0	Lace	Fingerling, Size 10 Crochet Thread	Steel 1.6-1.4mm/B-1	32-48
1	Superfine	Sock, Fingerling	2.25-3mm/B-1 to E-4	21-32
2	Fine	Sport, Baby	3.4-4.5mm/E-4 to 7	16-20
3	Light	DK, Light Worsted	4.5-5.5mm/7 to I/9	12-17
4	Medium	Worsted, Afghan, Aran	5.5-6.5mm/I-9 to K-10 ½	11-14
5	Bulky	Chunky, Craft, Rug	6.5-9mm/K-10 ½ to M-13	8-11
6	Super Bulky	Super Bulky, Roving	9-15mm/m-13 to Q	7-9
7	Jumbo	Jumbo, Roving	15mm and up	6 or more

Gauge

Gauge refers to the number of stitches across a row of four inches, and the number of rows in a four inch swatch of crochet fabric. Gauge is important to understand so that your projects will turn out correctly. In the table above we can see why using a medium weight yarn when a fine weight yarn is called for by the pattern will make your project much larger than you expected. Medium weight yarn typically has 11 to 14 stitches per four inch row, while fine weigh yarn has 16 to 20 stitches per four inch row.

Before you begin a pattern always take the time to work up a gauge swatch. Crochet a swatch using the yarn and hook size called for in the pattern. Then compare the swatch to the gauge of the pattern to see if you need to go up or down a hook size. If your swatch is too small then you will need to go up a hook size, and if it is too large you need to go down a hook size to obtain the correct gauge.

The following swatch was crocheted with a medium weight yarn and a size US I/9 (5.50mm) crochet hook. There are 13 stitch in a row of four inches, and 15 rows in a four inch square swatch.

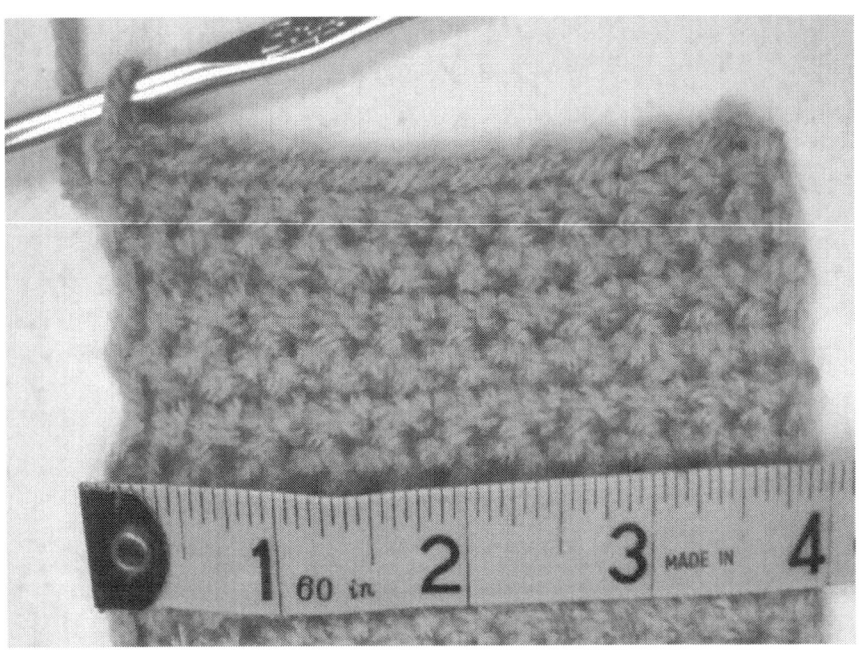

Yarn Labels

One of the best tools you have to choose the correct yarn for your projects is the yarn label. On the label you will find the fiber content, color, weight, recommended hook size, gauge, and laundry instruction symbols. Most yarn manufacturers use a standardized set of symbols on their yarn labels. You can find a complete list of laundry symbols on the Lion Brand website. I would recommend saving it and printing it out to take with you when you shop for yarn. Some yarn brands still use dye lots. A dye lot refers to a batch of yarn which was dyed in one lot. In other words all of the yarn with the same number was dyed together and the color will be consistent. If you purchase yarn with a dye lot, purchase more than you need of the same lot. That way the color will be consistent throughout your project.

In the following example we can see this is an acrylic yarn and the color is Cherry Red. The yarn weight is 4, or medium. The recommended hook size by the manufacturer is I/9 (5.50mm). This yarn may be machine washed and dried, but not ironed or bleached. This yarn will produce a four inch swatch with 12 stitches across the rows and 15 rows in four inches using the recommended hook size.

Crochet Hooks

Crochet hooks come in two main styles; inline and tapered. Inline hooks have a more defined sharp edge on the hook head, and tapered hooks are more curved. Both of these styles produce the same stitches. Which one you choose is a matter of preference. Personally I like tapered hooks, but some of my friends swear by their inline hooks. When working with a yarn that splits easily I find tapered hooks to be easier to use, but try both styles and decide which type you like the best.

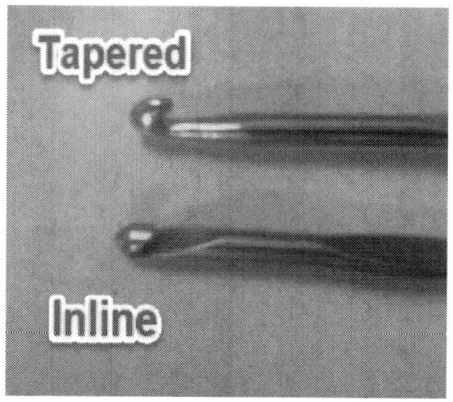

The crochet hook is made up of a handle, the grip, shaft, throat, and head. This is an example of Boye size I/9 hook. You may find different brands have slightly different grips and throats, but basically crochet hooks are all about the same in design. There are also ergonomic hooks which are easier to hold and don't cause as much stress to the hands. These hooks are great for people who have arthritis, carpal tunnel, or other conditions which may make holding a hook for long periods of time painful.

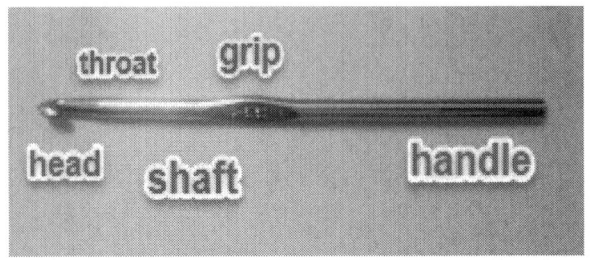

Most crochet hooks sold in the US have a number and letter designation. But you may find some hooks with only millimeter designations. Use the following table to help figure out crochet hook sizes.

US Size	Millimeter Size
B/1	2.25mm
C/2	2.75mm
D/3	3.25mm
E/4	3.5mm
F/5	3.75mm
G/6	4mm
7	4.5mm
H/8	5mm
I/9	5.5mm
J/10	6mm
K/10 ½	6.5mm
L/11	8mm
M-N/13	9mm
N-P/15	10mm
P/Q	15mm
Q	16mm
S	19mm

What You Need to Get Started

Basically all you need to crochet is a hook and yarn. I would recommend purchasing a good quality acrylic or wool blend yarn to practice with. You will also need a nice set of hooks. An aluminum set of hooks ranging from sizes E to K will serve you for a long time. You will also need a set of shears and some clip on stitch markers. Stitch markers are used to mark pattern repeats and the beginning of rounds of crochet. You can also get a row counter and a ball winder if you'd like. I know some crochet artists always wind their balls and skeins up before they use them to prevent knots and tangles, but that is up to you if you want to make these extra purchases.

CHAPTER TWO – Basic Crochet Stitches and Techniques

In this chapter we will go over the stitches and techniques you need to begin to crochet and work the patterns in this book. Grab a skein of yarn and a crochet hook and let's get started.

Chain Stitch

Create a slip knot and place it on the hook. Tighten it up so that the knot is snug, but not too tight. You still need to be able to get the hook and yarn through it. Place the yarn over the hook (known as a yarn over) and pull the yarn through the loop on the hook. This is a chain stitch. Yarn over and pull the yarn through the loop on the hook again. Now you have 2 chain stitches. Chain 12 stitches in total. Practice crocheting chain stitches until your stitches are nice and even. You want to keep your tension even and not too tight, or too loose. Your stitches should not sag or be very tight.

Most patterns begin with a line of chain stitches known as the foundation chain. When you feel comfortable with your chain stitches, make a chain of 12.

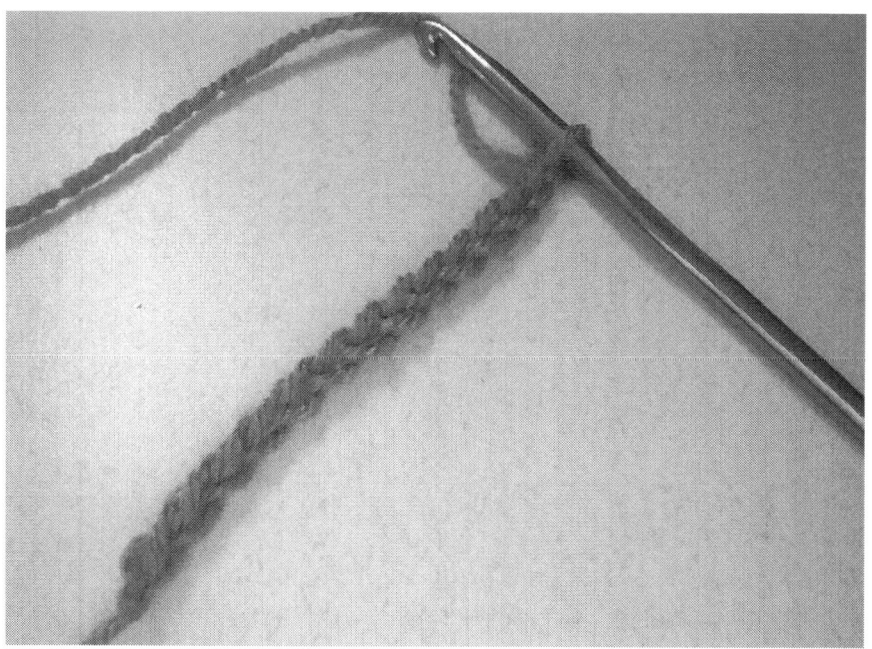

Practice until your stitches are nice and even.

Single Crochet

Single crochet gives you a dense fabric. If your first row is single crochet skip the first chain stitch from the hook and insert the hook into the second chain stitch. The first one is considered the first single crochet stitch. Yarn over and pull the yarn through the chain stitch. Now there are two loops on the hook. Yarn over and pull the yarn through both loops at once. This is a single crochet stitch. Insert the hook into the next chain stitch, yarn over and pull through the chain stitch, yarn over and pull through both loops on the hook. There are now three single crochet stitches in the row counting the first chain stitch. Continue across the row and when you get to the end of the row, turn your work after the last single crochet stitch.

To begin a new row of single crochet chain one. This chain one is considered and counted as the first single crochet stitch in the row. Insert the hook into the next stitch, not in the base of the chain one.

Yarn over and pull through the stitch. Yarn over and pull through both loops on the hook. You now have a chain one and a single crochet stitch in the second row. Work single crochet stitch in the remaining stitches across the row. When you come to the end, the last stitch is worked into the skipped chain stitch of the first row. On all subsequent rows the last stitch is worked into the chain one of the previous row. Practice single crochet stitches until your stitches are nice and even.

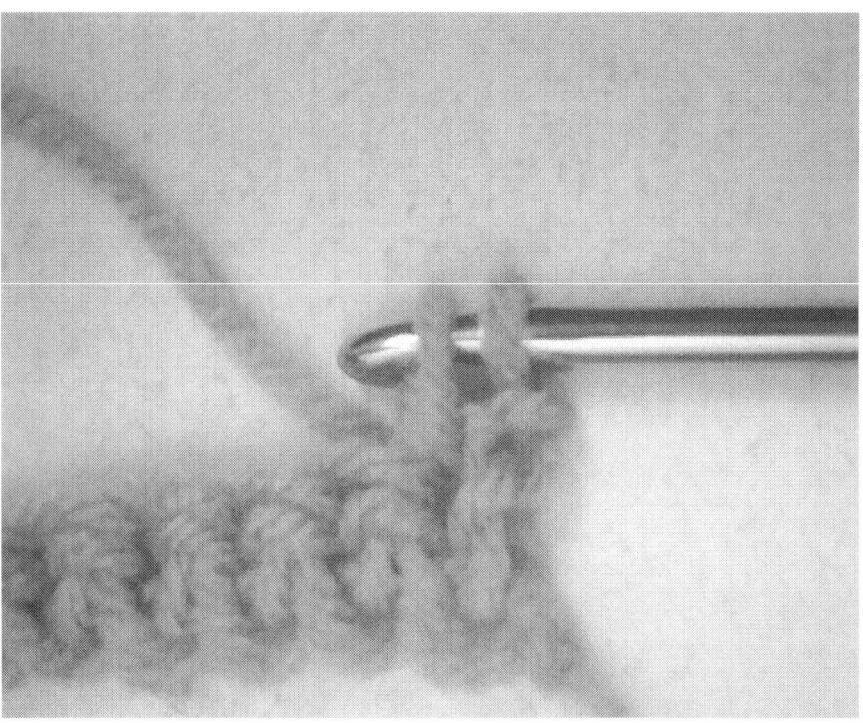

Chain 1 and insert the hook into the next stitch to begin the next row.

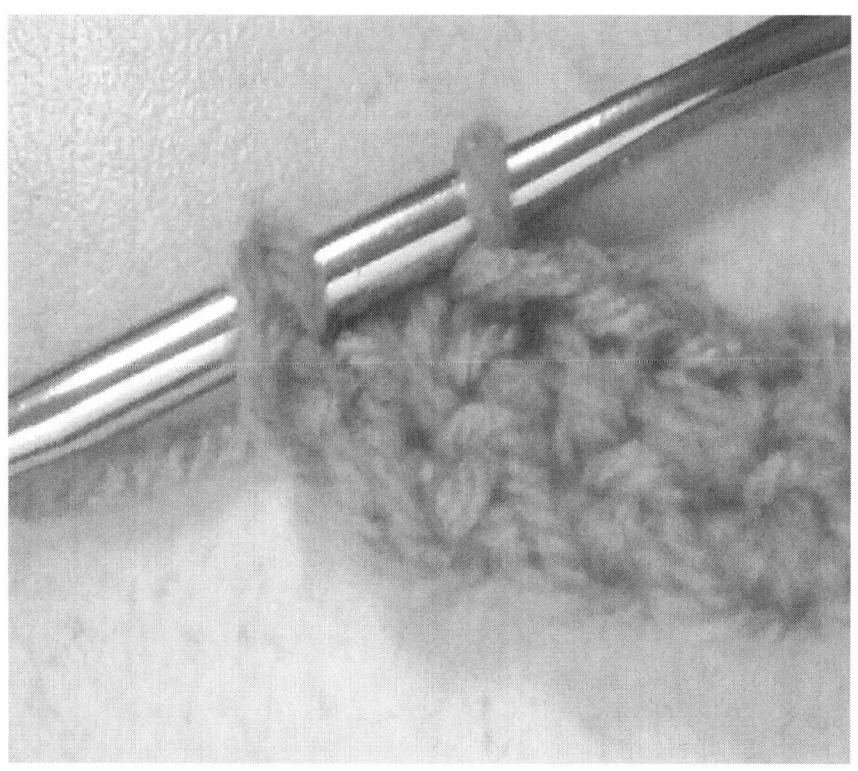

Work the last stitch into the skipped chain of the foundation chain, or chain one of the previous row.

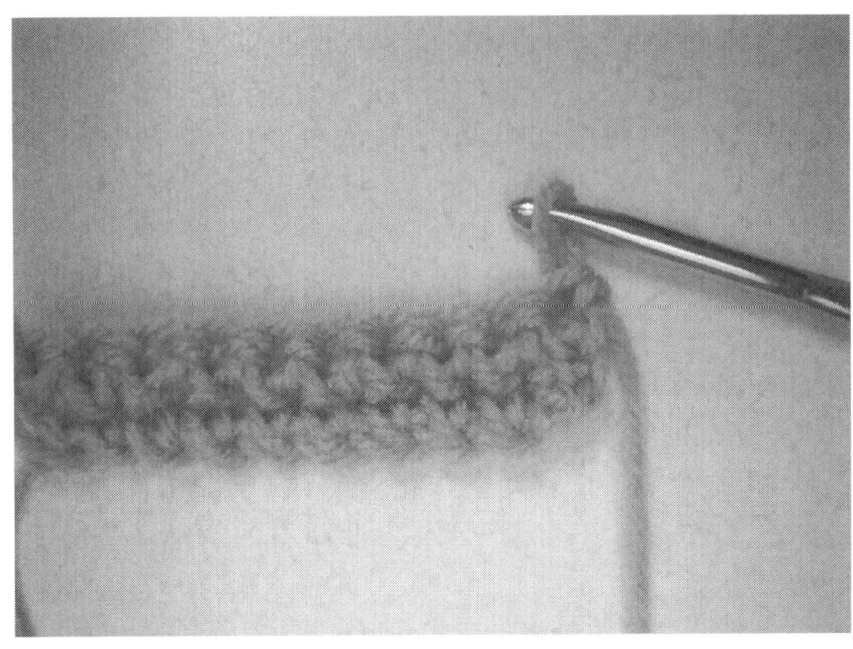

2 rows of single crochet

Double Crochet

The double crochet stitch produces a nice lofty fabric. It is used for the base of many other stitches such as the shell stitch, cluster stitch, and puff stitch. To begin a row of double crochet using a foundation chain skip three chain stitches and yarn over and insert the hook into the fourth chain from the hook. The three skipped chains are considered the first double crochet stitch of the row. Yarn over and pull the yarn through the chain stitch. Now you have three loops on the hook. Yarn over and pull through the first two loops. Now you have two loops left on the hook. Yarn over and pull through both loops at once to complete the stitch. Crochet double crochet stitches across the row and then turn your work.

To begin a new row of double crochet stitches chain three. These chains are considered and counted as the first double crochet stitch of the row. Yarn over and insert the hook into the next stitch, not the base of the chain three. Yarn over and pull through the stitch, yarn over and pull through the first two loops on the hook, and yarn over and pull through the last two loops on the hook to complete the stitch. Work your way across the row with double crochet stitches. The last stitch will be worked in the third chain stitch which was skipped on the foundation chain. At the end of each subsequent row the last stitch is worked into the third chain of the beginning chain three of the previous row.

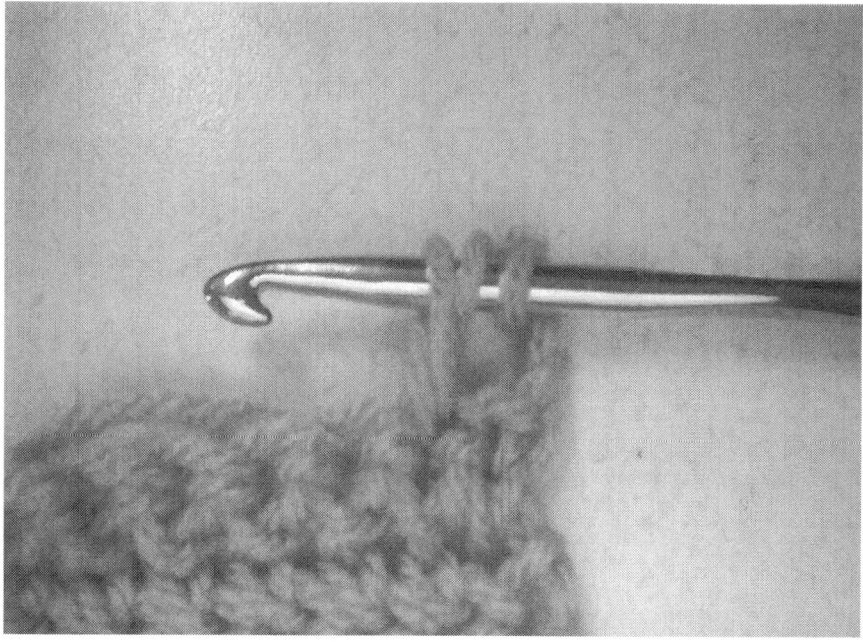

Yarn over and insert the hook into the next chain, yarn over and pull through the stitch.

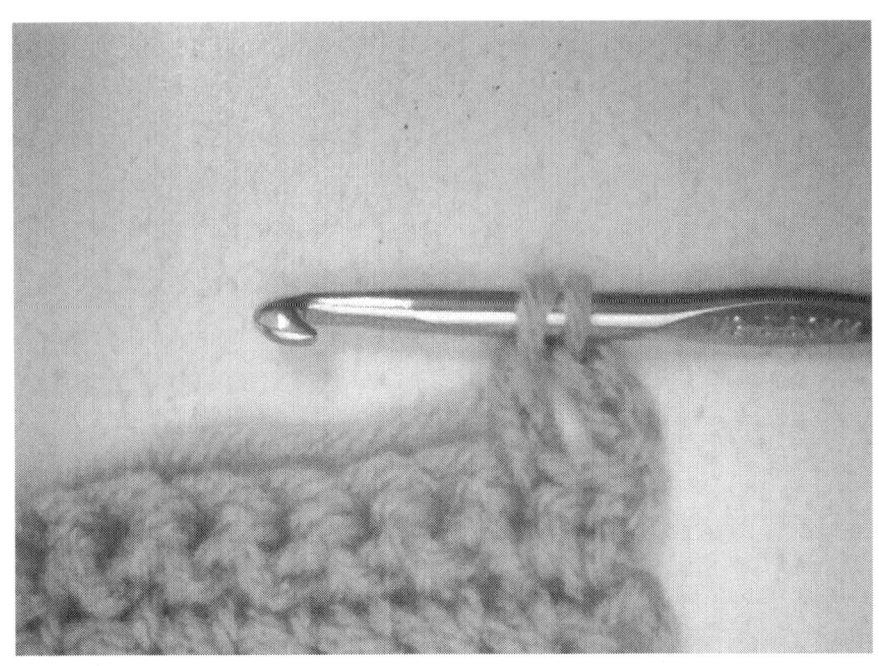

Yarn over and pull through the first 2 loops.

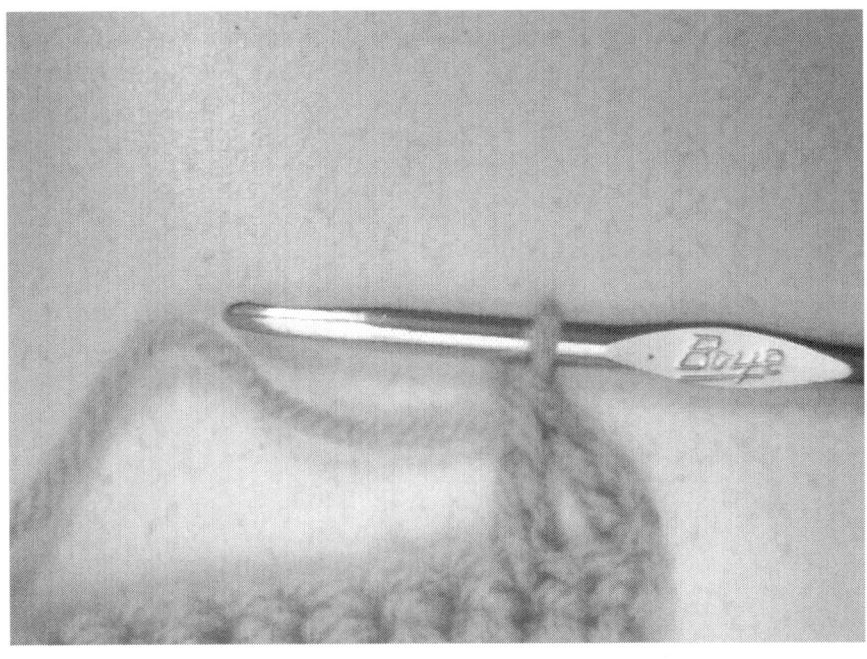

Yarn over and pull through the last 2 loops to complete the stitch.

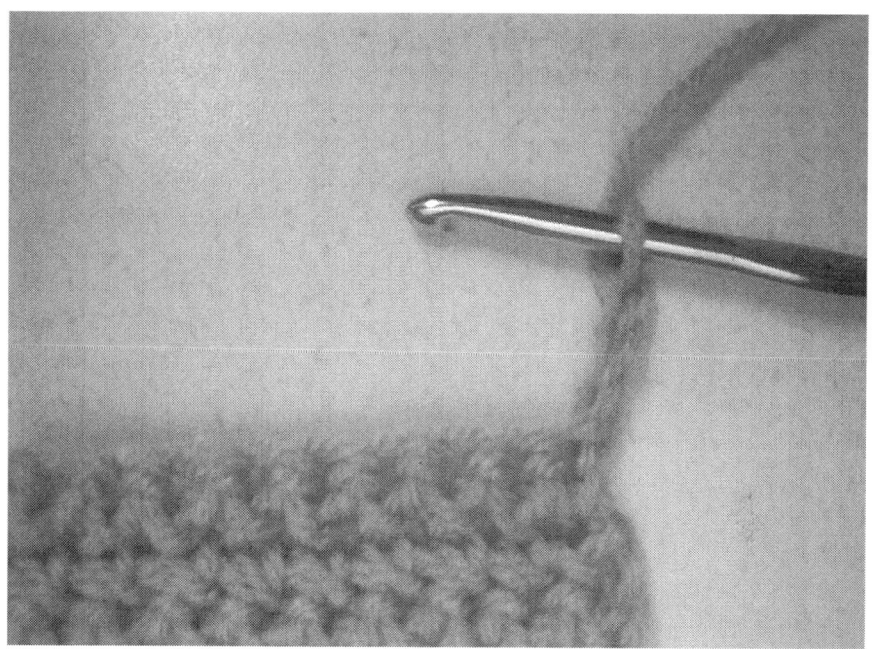

Chain 3 to begin a new row.

Half Double Crochet

The half double crochet is used a lot in hat patterns. It produces a dense fabric, but not as dense as the single crochet stitch. If you are starting out with a foundation chain, skip two chain stitches and yarn over the hook and insert the hook into the third chain stitch. The two skipped chain stitches are counted and considered as the first half double crochet stitch in the row. Yarn over and pull the yarn through the chain stitch. You now have three loops on the hook. Yarn over and pull the yarn through all three loops at once. To begin the next stitch yarn over and insert the hook into the next stitch. Yarn over and pull through the chain stitch, yarn over and pull through all three loops at once. Crochet half double crochet stitches across the starting chain and then turn your work.

To begin the next row chain two. These chains are considered the first half double crochet stitch in the row. Yarn over and insert the hook into the next stitch, not into the base of the chain two. Yarn over and pull through the stitch, yarn over and pull through all three loops on the hook at once. Crochet half double crochet stitches into all of the stitches in the row. When you get to the end the last stitch is worked into the skipped chain stitches of the foundation chain. In all subsequent rows you will chain two to begin and work the last stitch into the second chain of the starting chain of the previous row.

Treble Crochet

The treble crochet stitch is used to add height to stitch patterns. It produces a very loose fabric. To begin using a foundation chain skip five chain stitches. These are considered the first treble crochet stitch. Yarn over twice and insert the hook into the sixth chain from the hook. Yarn over and pull through the chain stitch. You now have four loops on the hook. Yarn over and pull through the first two loops. Yarn over and pull through the next two loops. Yarn over again and pull through the last two loops to complete the stitch. Crochet treble stitches across the foundation chain, work the last stitch in the fifth skipped chain, and turn your work.

To begin a new row chain five. These five chains are counted as the first treble crochet stitch. Yarn over twice and insert the hook into the next stitch, not the base of the chain five. Yarn over and pull through the stitch. Yarn over and pull through the first two loops, yarn over and pull through the next two loops, and yarn over once more and pull through the last two loops to finish the stitch. The last treble crochet stitch in the row is worked into the fifth chain of the starting chain of the previous row.

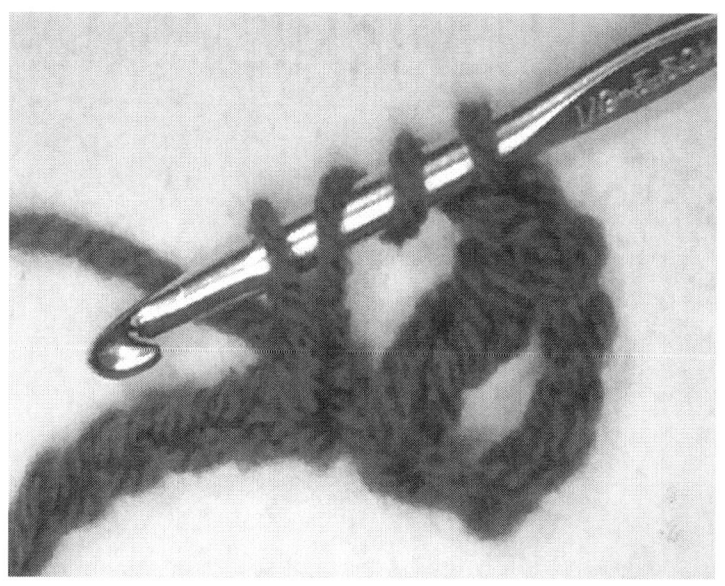

Yarn over twice and insert the hook into the next stitch, yarn over and pull through the stitch.

Yarn over and pull through two loops three times to complete the stitch.

Slip Stitch

The slip stitch is used to move the yarn to the proper place in a pattern, and to join rounds when crocheting in the round. No stitch is crocheted, you are just either moving the yarn or joining stitches. Insert the hook into the next stitch, yarn over and pull through the stitch and the loop on the hook.

Decreases

Sometimes in a pattern you will need to decrease the amount of stitches. This could be for shaping the crown of a hat, shaping the neckline of a garment, or to form the valleys of the ripple and chevron pattern. To decrease the stitch count by one you will need to crochet two stitches together. Begin a single crochet 2 together (sc2tog) by inserting the hook into the next stitch. Yarn over and pull through the stitch. Insert the hook into the next stitch, yarn over and pull through the stitch. There are now three loops on the hook. Yarn over and pull through all three loops at once. This crochets two single crochet stitches together and reduces the stitch count by one.

You can also use double crochet for a decrease. Yarn over and insert the hook into the next stitch, yarn over and pull through the stitch. Yarn over and pull through the first two loops on the hook. Yarn over and insert the hook into the next stitch, yarn over and pull through the stitch. Yarn over and pull through the first two loops on the hook, and then yarn over and pull through all three loops on the hook at once.

If you need to decrease the number of stitches by two, or create the valley of the ripple or chevron pattern, you will crochet three stitches together. The process is exactly the same but add one more stitch.

For example to crochet single crochet 3 together (sc3tog) insert the hook into the next stitch, yarn over and pull through. Insert the hook into the next stitch, yarn over and pull through. Insert the hook into the next stitch, yarn over and pull through (a total of three times). There are now four loops on the hook. Yarn over and pull through all four loops at once to complete the stitch.

To begin a double crochet three together (dc3tog) yarn over and insert the hook into the next stitch, yarn over and pull through the stitch. Yarn over and pull through the first two loops on the hook. Repeat this process twice more. You should have four loops on the hook. Yarn over and pull through all four loops at once. You will always end up with one more loop on the hook than stitches before your last yarn over and pull through step.

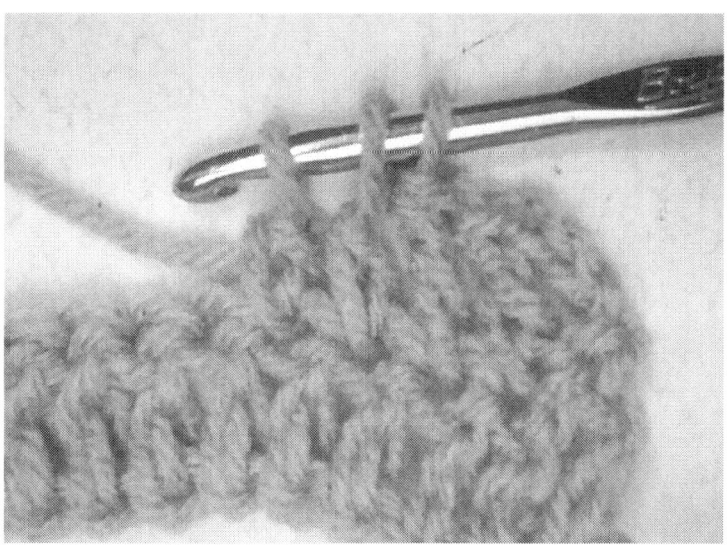

Dc2tog before the last yarn over and pull through

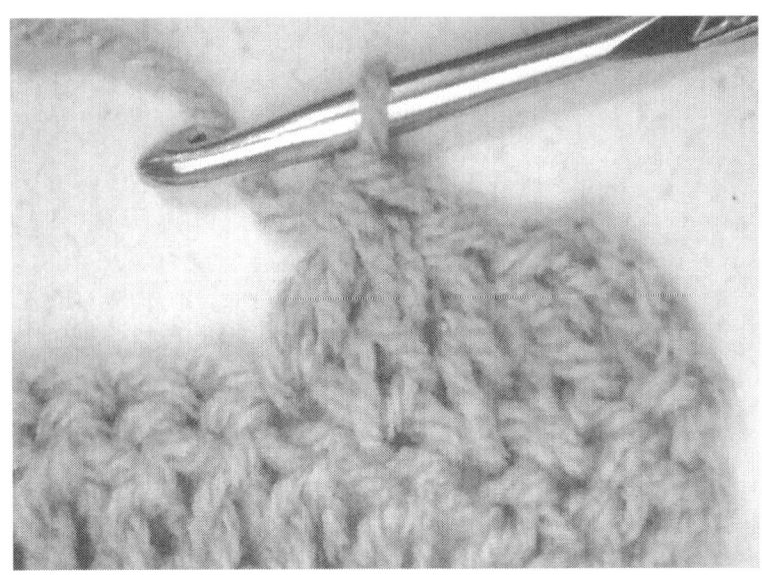

Completed dc2tog

Back and Front Loop Stitches

If you see blo or flo in a pattern this means you crochet in the back loop only or the front loop only. When you look at a crochet stitch you will see the very top two loops form a V shape. Normally you insert the hook under both of these two loops. But in back loop only stitches you insert the hook under the back loop, not both. The same goes for front loop stitches. Instead of inserting the hook under both loops of the next stitch, you would insert the hook under the front loop only. Back and front loops stitches are used to create a subtle ridge in the crochet fabric and are quite decorative.

Back loop double crochet (blodc)

Back and Front Post Stitches

If we look at a crochet stitch again we will see there is a post directly under the top of the stitch. It is this post that the hook wraps around for back and front post stitches. Back and front post stitches are used to create horizontal and vertical ridges in crochet. They are also used to create pretty decorative cables. The abbreviations for these stitches are bpdc (back post double crochet) and fpdc(front post double crochet).

To begin a back post double crochet yarn over and insert the hook from the back to the front around the post and back out the back of the stitch. Yarn over and pull the yarn around the post and even with the top of the other stitches in the row. Now complete the stitch as normal. I find it helps to pinch the fabric to make it easier to crochet a back post stitch. On the right side of the fabric back post stitches create a raised horizontal ridge.

Back post double crochet (bpdc)

To begin a front post double crochet yarn over and from the front insert the hook around the post coming back out in the front of the fabric. Yarn over and pull the yarn around the post and up even with the other stitches in the row. Complete the stitch as normal. On the right side of the fabric front post double crochet stitches create a vertical raised stitch.

Front post double crochet (fpdc)

Increases

Increases are also used to shape garments, hats, and form the peaks of ripple and chevron patterns. Increases are very easy. You simply crochet more than one stitch into a stitch. For example if you see 3sc into the next stitch you would crochet three single crochet stitches all into the next stitch. The same goes for double crochet, treble crochet, and half double crochet. You will usually see a number before a stitch denoting that many stitches should be worked into the next stitch. Here's what I mean:

Row 3: ch3, dc into each of the next 5 sts, 3dc into the next st, dc into each of the next sts, dc3tog...

This row would be worked by a chain three and a double crochet into each one of the next five stitches. Then you would crochet three double crochets all in the next stitch. One double crochet into each of the next five stitches, and then double crochet three together and so on according to the pattern.

Crochet Abbreviations

Designers use a standardized set of abbreviations when they write patterns. This is to make the patterns shorter and easier to understand. If a designer were to write out each and every term and instruction the pattern would be very long and confusing. Although a standardized set of abbreviations is used, sometimes a designer will have abbreviations or terms specific to their pattern. If they do they will include it in the key, special stitches, or notes. Always look for these items when beginning a pattern. The notes are included to help make the pattern easier to work as well as any information the designer may have thought would be helpful.

The following table contains the most common abbreviations and their meanings in US terms.

Stitch Name	Abbreviation
Chain stitch	Ch
Stitch/Stitches	St/sts
Slip stitch	Sl st
Single crochet	Sc
Double crochet	Dc
Half double crochet	Hdc
Treble crochet	Trb
Repeat	Rep
Single crochet 2 together	Sc2tog
Double crochet 2 together	Dc2tog
Half double crochet 2 together	Hdc2tog

You may also find patterns written in UK terms. These take a bit of translation to work. Use the following table to help translate UK terms to US terms.

US Terms		UK Terms	
Chain	Ch	Chain	Ch
Slip stitch	Sl st	Slip stitch	Ss
Single crochet	Sc	Double crochet	Dc
Half double crochet	Hdc	Half treble	Htr
Double crochet	Dc	Treble	Tr
Treble crochet	Trb	Double treble	dtr

Working with Patterns

Working with written patterns is a very good skill to learn. Patterns are actually quite easy once you understand how they are laid out. Most designers include the abbreviations used on the pattern. Check these out to make sure you know all of the stitches. Next look for the type and color of yarn you will need. You can substitute colors and brands of yarn as long as they are the same weight and fiber type. Look for the size of hook, or hooks, you will need to complete the pattern. Note if there are any special stitches or notes given by the designer.

Now look at the pattern itself. It is a good practice to read over a pattern before you begin to work it to be sure you understand all of the instructions. Read the pattern line by line. Once you feel familiar with the pattern, then it is time to actually start to crochet it. Take your time and don't try to skip ahead or rush. If you have to rip out your work, don't feel bad, we all have to do this sometimes. Ripping out stitches is known as "frogging" in crochet slang.

For now stick with beginner or easy patterns. As you grow in confidence and skill you can take on more complicated patterns. After the first couple of patterns you'll be a pro at reading and working them.

Crocheting in the Round

When you crochet a hat or a motif you will probably be crocheting in the round. Instead of going back and forth in rows you actually go around in rounds. Most crochet in the round projects begin with a starting chain which is joined to form a ring. You may work into the stitches of the joined starting chain, or into the center of the chain around the stitches. Your pattern will tell you which method to use. For example a Granny square begins with chain three or four. The chains are joined by inserting the hook back into the first chain, yarn over and pull through the chain stitch and the loop on the hook. The first round of stitches is worked into the center of the ring, not into the actual stitches themselves. The round is then joined with slip stitch.

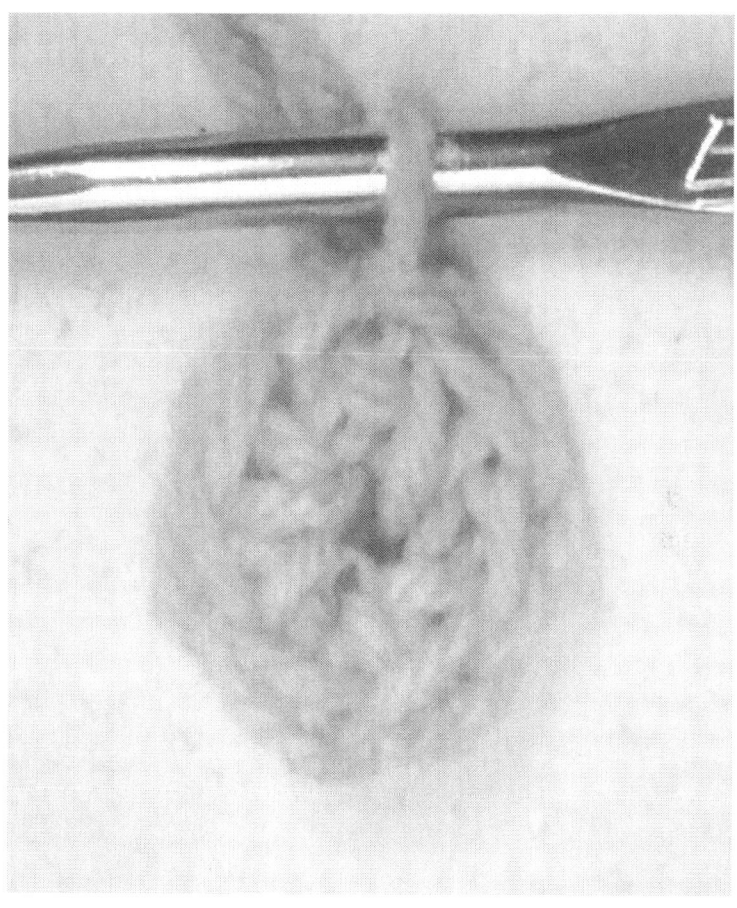

First round joined

When you work in the round it is a good practice to place a stitch marker at the beginning of the round. When you complete the round move the stitch marker up to the starting chain of the next round so that you will know when to join and complete the round. This is especially important when crocheting single crochet since the stitches are short and it is hard to tell when the round stops and the next one should begin.

Most of the time you will not turn your work when working in the round unless the pattern instructs you to do so. Once exception is Granny squares. Granny squares naturally lean in the middle because of the tension of the yarn and the way the stitches come together. You can remedy this by turning your work after each round. Then you will end up with a nice straight middle to your Granny squares.

Color Changes

Color changes are quite easy in crochet. Work the last stitch of the old color until you have two loops on the hook. Grab the new color and pull through these two loops and then continue on with the new color. When changing colors at the end of a row, work the last stitch in the row until there are two loops on the hook. Pick up the new color and draw it through the two loops. When you chain to begin a new row, capture the old color in the first chain stitch to secure it.

If you are coming back across the row and changing back to the old color don't cut it (fasten off), let it rest at the beginning of the row and then pull it through the last two loops of the last stitch of the row. Capture the old color in the first chain stitch of the new row and let it rest there until you come back for it. By carrying the colors up the side of the fabric you reduce the number of tails you have to weave in.

Work the last stitch until there are 2 loops on the hook.

Color change completed

Example of carrying the colors up the side of the fabric

When changing color in the row itself the process is the same. Work the last stitch of the old color until there are two loops on the hook. Pull the new color through the two loops, place the old color over the new color for one stitch, and continue to crochet. By capturing the old color in the first stitch of the new color you secure the yarn and make it less likely to work its way out even after weaving in the tail. Now you can cut (fasten off) the old color leaving at least a six inch tail. Always leave at least six inches when fastening off the yarn so you can weave it in securely.

Work the old color to the last 2 loops of the stitch

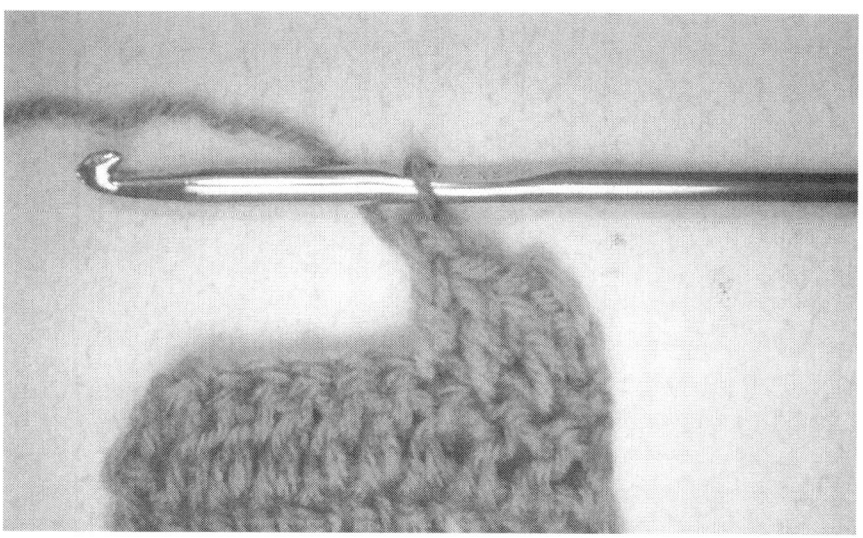

Pull the new color through the last 2 loops

Color change completed

Weaving in Tails

When you cut, or fasten off, yarn leave at least six inches. This gives you a nice long tail to weave in. You don't want to put all your time and effort into a project only to have the ends work their way out of the stitches and start to unravel. I like to weave in the tails as I go. Facing all of the loose tails at the end of a project is just not a favorite thing to do, but if you want to wait and weave in the tails all at once that is fine.

First be sure all of the tails are pulled to the wrong side of the fabric, or inside if you're crocheting in the round. Thread a tapestry, or blunt end, needle with the tail. Weave in and out of the stitches for about an inch. Turn the fabric and weave in and out for another inch going in a different direction. Turn the fabric once more and weave in and out of the stitches for another inch going another way. Now you can safely cut the yarn and not worry about the tails working their way out of the stitches.

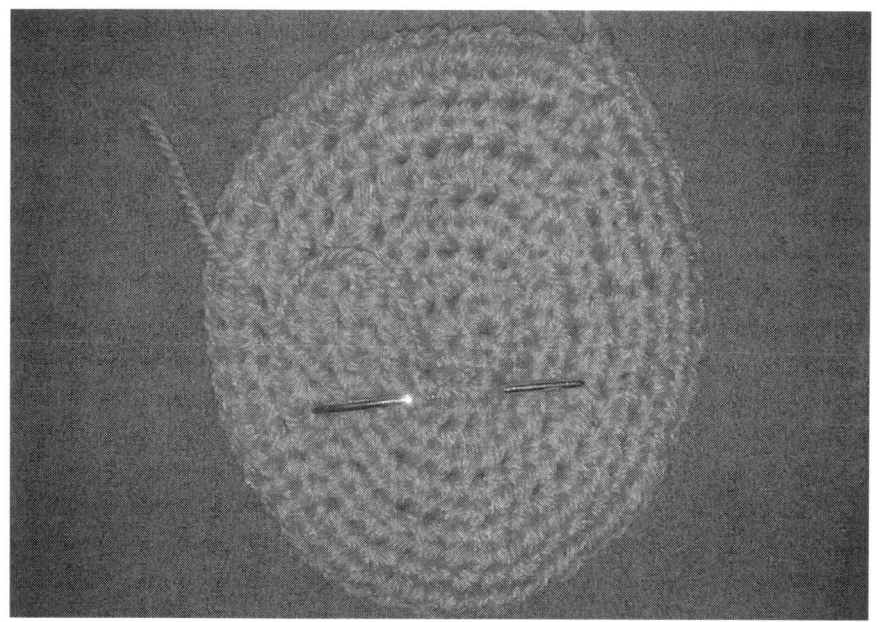

Tips for Nice Clean and Straight Edges

One of the most important habits you can get into is to count your stitches as you work. Crochet is based upon stitch counts, and if the count is off in one row the rest of the project will be off. Always end the row with the last stitch worked in the top of the turning chain. The turning chain is the chain one, chain two, chain three, or chain five you crochet to begin a new row. Unless the pattern specifies it crochet the first stitch after the turning chain in the stitch right next to it, not in the base of the chain.

Count the turning chain as the first stitch. For example if you the pattern tells you to chain 3 and then work 11 double crochet across the row for a total of 12 stitches, remember the chain 3 counts as a double crochet. By counting your stitches you can keep your edges nice and straight and always have the correct number of stitches in each row or round.

Planning a Project

Probably the first thing you think of when you want to plan a project is the color. There are lots of colors and color schemes to choose from. You can pick a complimentary color scheme such as oranges and blues, or one that is the same color but in different shades such as violet, lavender, and light purple. You may choose a primary color scheme with red, blue, and yellow. Secondary colors include green, purple, and orange.

Warm colors include orange, orange/red, yellow, and brown. A cool palette includes blue, violet, and red. In a cool scheme the red and green will have a blue undertone while in a warm scheme the red and green will have more of a yellow or orange undertone. Here is an illustration of the color wheel to help you choose your colors. (Don't feel bound by the color wheel, though. Use the colors you like.)

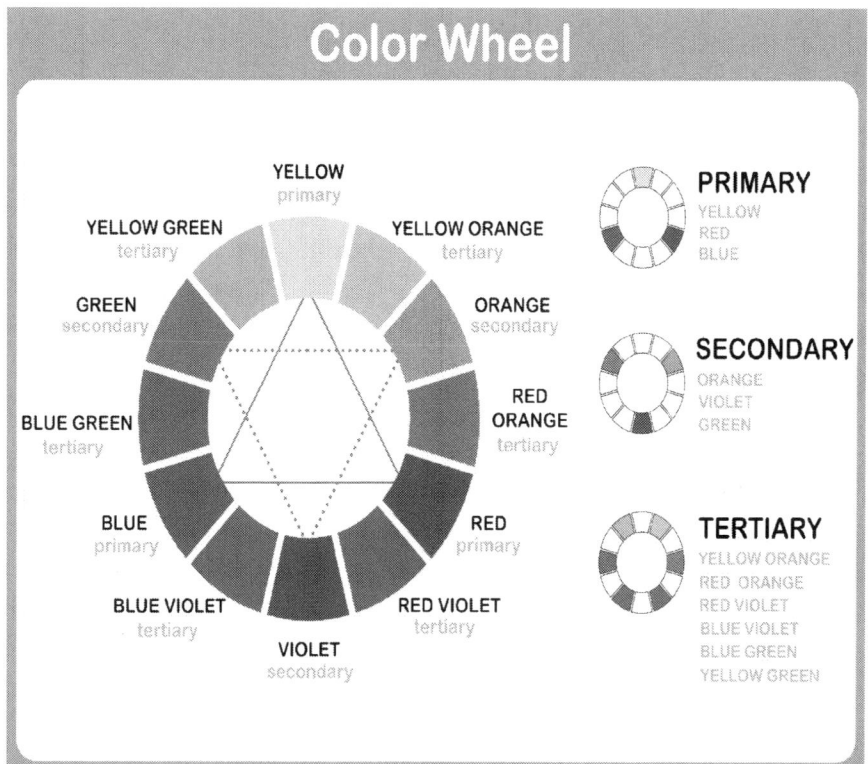

Next decide on how large you want your afghan to be. Are you making a baby blanket or an afghan to fit a double size bed? Once you decide on how large you want your project to be check the following table for the correct measurements. For example if you want to crochet a baby or crib blanket your afghan will need to be 30 inches by 54 inches. This is where a gauge swatch comes in handy.

Use the yarn and crochet hook you plan on making the afghan with and crochet up a gauge swatch at least four inches square. Count the number of stitches across four inches in a row and write that number down. Now count the rows it takes to make four inches and write that number down. Let's say you came up with 12 stitches in across the row in four inches. This means each inch has 3 stitches in it.

And say you have 16 fours in four inches. This means it takes 4 rows to make an inch. So you have 4 rows and 3 stitches per inch.

How to Figure Out the Length of the Foundation Chain

This means for 30 inches wide you will need 90 stitches (30 inches times 3 stitches), and to make the blanket 54 inches long you will need 216 rows (54 inches times 4 rows). Most patterns have a set number of stitches they use to form the pattern. For example let's say the ripple pattern you want to use has a foundation chain which needs to be in sets of 10. This works out perfectly because you need 90 stitches in your foundation chain to make 30 inches. So when you start to crochet the pattern you will be repeating the stitch pattern nine times across the foundation chain and in all of rows of the afghan. You can use a row counter or a pencil and a piece of paper to keep track of the rows until you reach 216, or 54 inches.

How to Figure Out How Many Granny Squares You Will Need for a Project

Figuring out how many squares you need for a project is even easier than figuring out a foundation chain. Crochet a Granny square and measure its length and width. It should be square, say for example four inches square. Look at the table to choose the size of project you want to make. Let's say for example you want to crochet up a pretty bedspread for a double bed. That means your completed project will be at least 60 inches wide and 78 inches long. Take the width, 60 inches, and divide it by the size of the square, 4 inches. The answer is 15, so you will need 15 Granny squares across the width of the afghan. Now take the length, 78 inches, and divide it by the size of the square, 4 inches. The answer is 19 ½, but you would round up to 20. The afghan will be 20 squares long. Now take the number of squares you need for the width, 15, and multiply it by the number of squares for the length, 20. The answer is 300. You will need 300, 4 inch squares to complete an afghan to fit a double size bed. Don't worry about the joining measurements. As long as you make the correct number of squares the joining won't add that much width or length to the project.

Afghan and Throw Size Chart	
Size	**Measurements**
Crib	30 x 54 inches
Lapghan	36 x 48 inches
Twin Bed	48 x 78 inches
Long Twin Bed	48 x 84 inches
Double Bed	60 x 78 inches
Queen Size Bed	66 x 84 inches
King Size Bed	80 x 84 inches

Now that you know how long the foundation chain must be, or how many Granny squares you will need, you are ready to start to crochet.

CHAPTER THREE – Granny Square Basics

The Granny square afghan is what most people think of when they think of crochet. And this is for good reason. The Granny square has been a favorite for many decades. In this chapter we'll learn how to crochet a Granny square and in the next chapters we'll learn some variations on this time honored motif. Later we will also discuss a few ways to join the squares once you get the completed. I will also give you tips on how to create a perfectly straight Granny square and show an example of a giant Granny square that I crocheted and use as an afghan.

You can use the colors I do, or you can substitute any color combination you like. That is one of the fun things about Granny squares – all the different color combinations you can come up with. One of the most attractive, in my opinion, and fun types of Granny square afghan is to use the bits of leftover yarn in your stash. Each square is a different color combination and is joined with a single color to pull it all together.

How to Crochet a Granny Square

Granny squares are crocheted in the round. First chain 4 and join with a slip stitch in the first chain to form a ring. The first round of stitches is not crocheted into the 4 chain stitches, but into the center of the ring.

Chain 3 and crochet 2 double crochet. The chain 3 counts as the first double crochet. Chain 1 and then crochet 3 more double crochet. Chain 1 and crochet 3 more double crochet twice more. Join with a slip stitch into the 3rd chain of the starting chain (the first chain 3).

Round 1

If you are changing colors for the next round cut the yarn and leave a long tail to weave in later. Make a slip knot and place it on your hook. Insert the hook into a chain 3 space and join the new color with a slip knot.

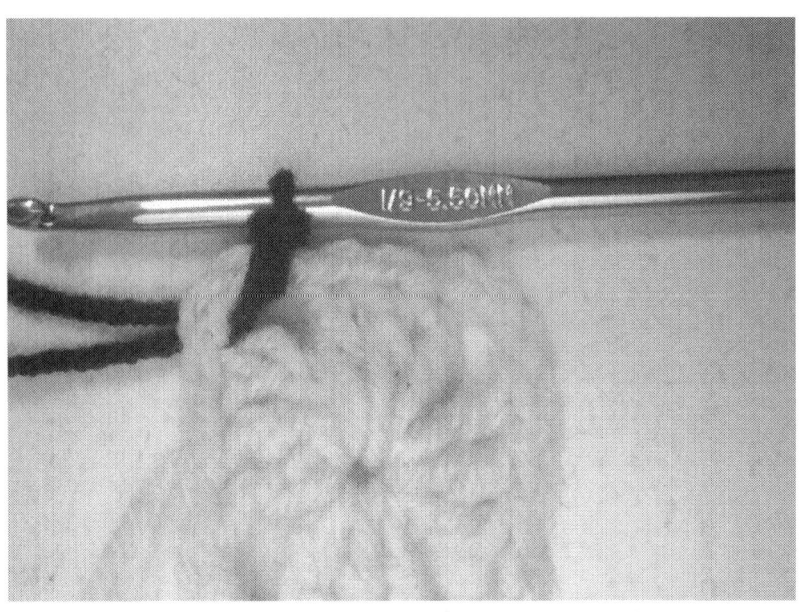

Joining a new color

If you are not changing colors slip stitch to the next chain 3 space. This will position your yarn in the correct space to begin the next round. Chain 3, crochet 2 more double crochet and chain 3. Crochet 3 more double crochet into the same chain 3 space. This is the first corner. Chain 1, into the next chain 3 space work 3 double crochet, chain 3, and 3 double crochet. Chain 1 and into the next chain 3 space work 3 double crochet, chain 3, and 3 double crochet. Repeat this again in the last chain 3 space, chain 1 and join with a slip stitch into the 3rd chain of the starting chain. You should have four sets of 3 double crochet, chain 3, 3 double crochet separated by a chain 1.

Round 2

To begin the third round either join a new color or slip stitch to the next chain 3 space. Chain 3 and crochet 2 double crochet, chain 3, and 2 double crochet into the first chain 3 space. Chain 1 and work 3 double crochet chain 1 into the next chain 1 space. Work around the square crocheting 3 double crochet, chain 3, 3 double crochet, chain 1 into each chain 3 space (corners), and 3 double crochet, chain 1 into each chain 1 space.

3 round Granny square

You can make your squares as large or as small as you like. Just keep fastening off the yarn and joining a new color into a chain 3 space, or slip stitch to the first chain 3 space to begin a new round. If you want your square to be perfectly straight, turn the square after each round and do not slip stitch to the next chain 3 space. This will prevent the natural lean that occurs in the middle of larger Granny squares. If you're only going to make your squares three or four rounds big, you won't really have to worry about the lean. It usually occurs in larger squares.

Here are a few examples of Granny square projects:

For this project Granny squares were combined with rows of Granny shells. Notice how the crochet artist used different sizes of squares and coordinating colors to bring out the design.

Here is an example of a large afghan sized Granny square. Notice the typical lean of the inside rounds.

CHAPTER FOUR – Granny Square Variations

The Granny square lends itself to variations very easily. In this chapter we will learn three Granny Square variations. Each one is based on the basic Granny square, but uses stitches in different combinations. I am going to work up two squares of each variation, plus two basic Grannies, so that I can teach you how to join them in the next chapter. I would suggest you do the same so you can follow along once we start to join the squares.

Solid Granny Square

One of the easiest variations is the solid Granny. Begin by chaining 4 and joining with a slip stitch into the first chain to form a ring. Chain 3 and crochet 4 double crochet. Chain 1, crochet 5 double crochet, and repeat chain 1, 5 double crochet twice more. Chain 1 and join in the 3rd starting chain.

What you have done is substituted the chain 3 of a corner in a traditional Granny square with a double crochet, chain1, double crochet. Compare the traditional Granny square you crocheted in the last section with the solid one you just finished. Notice how the corners are different. This is the major difference between a solid Granny and a traditional motif.

Add rounds by either joining a new color in a chain 1 space, slip stitching to the first chain1 space, or turning the square and then slip stitching to the first chain 1 space. Chain 4, and double crochet into the chain 1 space. The beginning chain 4 counts as the first double crochet and chain 1. Crochet a double crochet into each double crochet across the side. When you reach the next chain 1 space, work a double crochet, chain 1, double crochet into it. Crochet a double crochet into each double crochet stitch on the side and double crochet, chain 1, double crochet into each corner around the square. Join with a slip stitch into the 3rd beginning chain.

Repeat this for each round. Remember to join the new color, or slip stitch, to the first chain 1 space. You will chain 4 and double crochet into the first chain 1 space. Then work a double crochet into each double crochet stitch along the side. Each chain 1 space is worked with a double crochet, chain 1, double crochet.

Work your way around the square and join in the 3rd beginning chain. Your rounds will increase by 2 stitches on each side as the square grows. For example the first round has 5 double crochet across the sides separated by a chain 1. The second round has 7 double crochet across the sides separated by a chain 1. The third round has 9, the fourth 11, and so on.

Round Center Granny Square

To begin chain 4 and join in the first chain with a slip stitch. Chain 3 and crochet 15 double crochet into the ring, join in the 3rd chain of the starting chain. You should have 16 stiches. Fasten off and leave a long tail to weave in later.

Join the next color in any stitch. You will be working into the stitches of the first round. Chain 3, 2 double crochet into the same space. Half double crochet into the next stitch, single crochet into the next stitch, half double crochet into the next stitch. Repeat the following pattern of stitches around: 3 double crochet into the same stitch, half double crochet into the next stitch, single crochet into the next stitch, double crochet into the next stitch. Join in the 3rd chain of the starting chain. Fasten off and leave a long tail to weave in later. This round makes the motif a square.

Join the next color in the second double crochet of a corner shell. Chain 3, crochet 2 double crochet into the same space. Chain 1, work 3 double crochet into the same space. Chain 1, work 3 double crochet into the next single crochet, chain 1. Repeat the following stitch pattern around: 3 double crochet, chain 1, 3 double crochet into the 2nd double crochet of the next corner shell, chain 1, 3 double crochet into the next single crochet, chain1. Join in the 3rd chain of the starting chain. Fasten off and leave a long tail to weave in later.

To add more rounds join the next color in the chain1 space of a corner. Chain 3 and work 2 double crochet, chain 3, 3 double crochet into the same space. Chain 1, work 3 double crochet and chain 1 into the next chain1 space. Continue around the square working 3 double crochet and chain 1 into each chain 1 space. In the corner spaces work 3 double crochet, chain 3, 3 double crochet, chain1. Join in the 3rd chain of the starting chain. Fasten off and leave a long tail to weave in later. 3

Drop Stitch Granny Square

This variation of the Granny square uses the drop stitch to create a very unique look. Begin by chaining 4 and joining the chain in the first chain with a slip stitch. Crochet the first round exactly like a basic Granny square. Fasten off the yarn and leave a long tail to weave in later.

Join the next color in any chain 3 space. Chain 3, work 2 double crochet and chain 1. The drop stitch is crocheted just like a double crochet, but instead of inserting the hook into the chain three space, insert it into the center of the starting ring. Yarn over and pull the yarn up even with the top of the other stitches in round 2. Yarn over and pull through the two loops on the hook to complete the stitch. Chain 1 and work 3 double crochet into the same chain 3 space. Chain 1. Repeat this pattern around the square: 3 double crochet, chain 1, drop stitch, chain 1, 3 double crochet, chain 1. Join in the 3rd chain of the starting chain, fasten off and leave a long tail to weave in later.

Join the next color in the first chain 1 space of a corner. Chain 3, 2double crochet in the same space, Chain 3, 3 double crochet into the next chain 1 space. Chain 1, In the next chain 1 space work a double crochet, work a drop stitch by inserting the hook into the 2nd double crochet of the shell in the previous round, double crochet and chain 1. Repeat this pattern around the square: At the corners work 3 double crochet into the first chain 1 space. Chain 3. Work 3 double crochet into the next chain 1 space of the corner and chain 1. In the next chain 1 space on the side work a double crochet, a drop stitch into the 2nd double crochet of the shell in the previous row, another double crochet into the chain 1 space, and chain 1. Join into the 3rd chain of the starting chain, fasten off and leave a long tail to weave in later.

To add more rounds alternate working a drop stitch in the corner and on the sides.

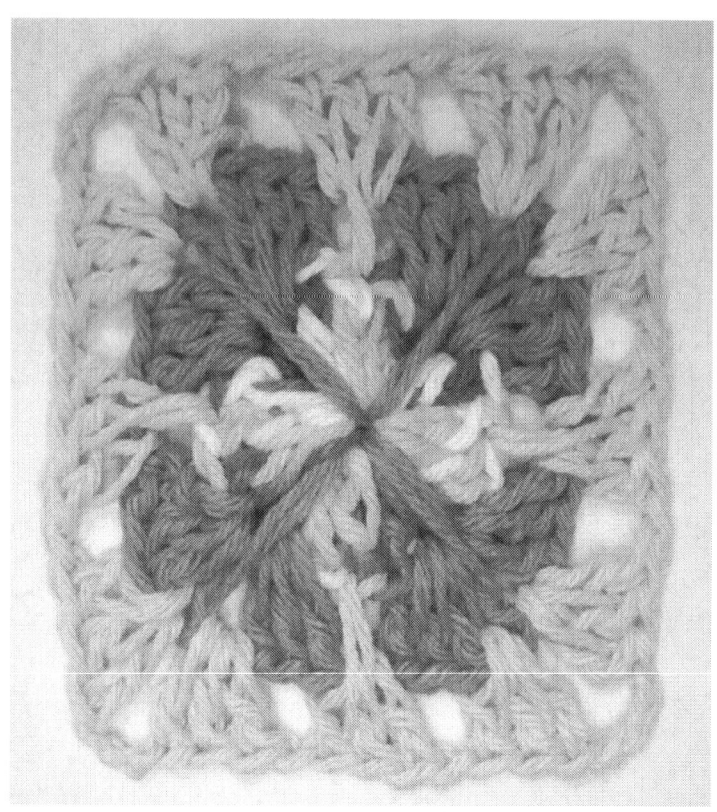

CHAPTER FIVE – Joining Methods

There are several ways you can join your Granny squares and other motifs you have crocheted. In this chapter we'll learn three simple joining methods; whip stitch, single crochet, and slip stitch. Take the eight squares you have crocheted and arrange them into two sets of four. We will join the sets of four and then crochet the sets together to create a cute pot holder.

Whip Stitch Method

The whip stitch method creates a slight braided effect between the squares. Cut a long piece of yarn and thread a tapestry or blunt end needle with either a contrasting or matching color of yarn. I am using off white so that you can see the work better, but if I were going to join them for a personal project I would use a matching color of yarn.

Hold two squares together with the right side facing each other. Line up the stitches on the edges of the squares. Insert the needle into the outer loops of the corner stitches and draw the yarn up through the stitches leaving a long tail to weave in. Insert the needle into the outer loops of each set of outer stitches across the square. When you reach the other end, pick up two more squares with the right sides facing and whip stitch across these squares in the same manner. When you reach the end of the squares, fasten off and leave a long tail to weave in later.

Fold the squares so that the right sides are together and sew up the other seam. Remember to only catch the outer loops of the stitches when sewing. When you reach the corner where all four squares join whip stitch under the whip stitch of the previous seam. Fasten off and leave a long tail to weave in.

Weave in the tails before you join the other four squares.

Catch only the outer loops of the stitches

Close up of the whip stitch join method

Slip Stitch Method

The slip stitch method uses slip stitches to join the squares. Hold two squares with the wrong sides facing and join the yarn into a corner. Chain 1. Slip stitch into each stitch across the square catching both edge stitches in the slip stitch. When you reach the other corner slip stitch into the corner, pick up the other two squares holding them wrong sides facing and slip stitch into the next corner space. Slip stich across the edges of the squares and end with two slip stitches in the last corner space. Fasten off and leave a long tail to weave in.

Fold the squares together with wrong sides facing and slip stitch along the edges to join. Then you reach the corner where all four squares meet, slip stitch under the corner stitch. Fasten off and leave a long tail when you reach the end. Weave in the tails. The slip stitch method creates a raised ridge on the right side of the fabric. You can slip stitch on the wrong side if you don't want the ridge to show.

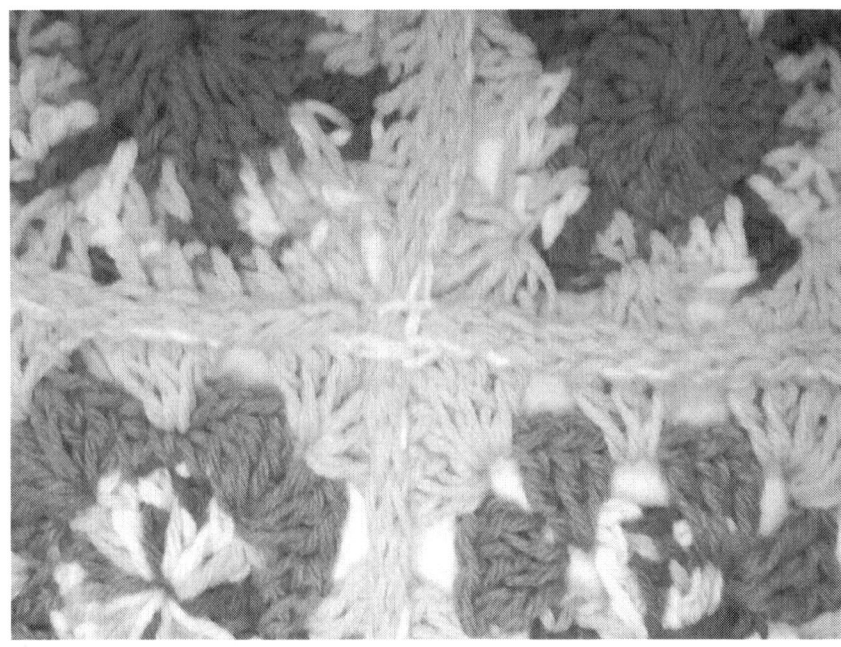

Single Crochet Method

The single crochet joining method is one of my favorite. It creates a pretty frame around each square and can add a lot of interest and texture to your afghan. For this example we will be joining the two sets of four squares to create a double thickness. Hold the squares wrong sides together and join the yarn in any corner. Chain 1. Single crochet across the edges of both squares matching up the stitches and the seams. Be sure to catch the edge stitches of both squares in the single crochet stitches to join the pieces. Here is what the first seam looks like to give you an idea of how the single crochet method works up for joining motifs.

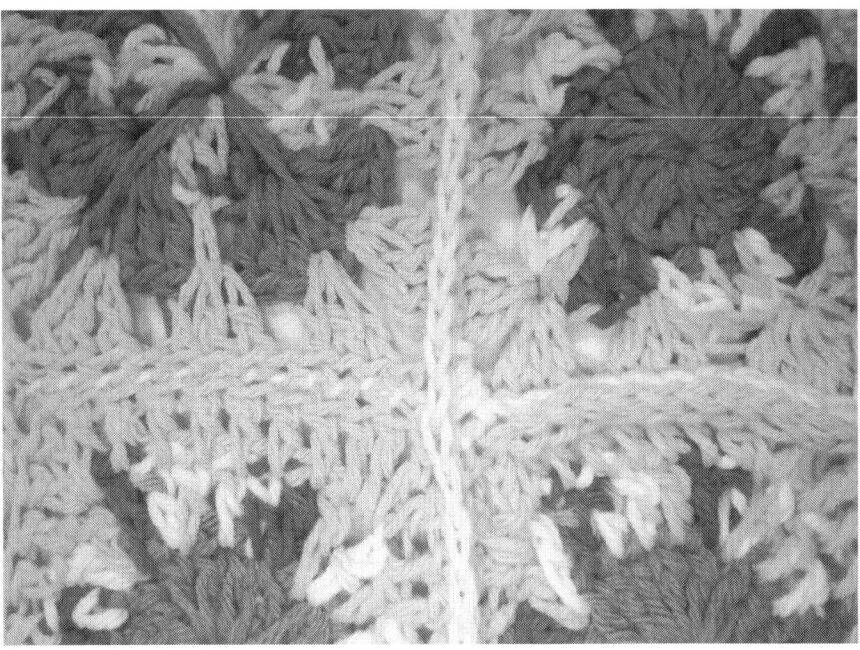

In this example you can see the vertical seam is single crochet. Notice how it creates a raised frame. On the left is the whip stitch join, and on the right is the slip stitch join. This is a good image to help you visualize how each method looks and to compare them

Continue to single crochet around the edge of the two pieces working 3 double crochet into each corner space. When you have crocheted all of the way around, join in the chain 1, fasten off the yarn and weave in the tails. Now you have an attractive and useful potholder.

You can use any of these three joining methods when crocheting a Granny Square afghan.

Slip stitch side of potholder

Whip stich side of potholder

Thank you for purchasing this book on learning how to crochet, and how to crochet Granny squares and joining methods. With the skills in this book you are well on your way to creating beautiful heirloom projects for family and friends. If you like this book, please consider leaving a review on Amazon. Thanks!

69717218R00075

Made in the USA
San Bernardino, CA
20 February 2018